D0262327

Visual Sources Series

THE TWENTIETH CENTURY 1914–1970

Peter Lane
Principal Lecturer in History,
Coloma College of Education

B. T. BATSFORD London

Visual Sources Series
1   The Industrial Revolution 1750–1830
2   The Victorian Age 1830–1914
3   The Twentieth Century 1914–1970

First published 1972
© Peter Lane, 1972

ISBN 0 7134 1722 6

Filmset by Keyspools Ltd, Golborne, Lancs.

Printed in Great Britain by The Anchor Press, Tiptree, Essex
for the Publishers
B. T. Batsford Ltd, 4 Fitzhardinge Street, London W1H OAH

Contents

The Illustrations

Acknowledgment

The author and the publishers wish to thank the following for permission to reproduce illustrations in this book: Aerated Bread Co. for Chapter 8 fig. 6; Aerofilms Ltd. for Chapter 2 fig. 7, Chapter 4 figs. 3, 4, Chapter 5 fig. 3, Chapter 11 fig. 3; Associated Newspapers for Chapter 8 fig. 2; British Leyland Motor Corporation for Chapter 2 fig. 3, Chapter 4 fig. 1; BOAC for Chapter 4 figs. 5, 6; BBC for Chapter 11 fig. 2; British Steel Corporation for Chapter 6 fig. 5; the Bowater Organisation for Chapter 8 fig. 8; Montague Burton Ltd. for Chapter 1 fig. 3; Central Office of Information (Crown copyright reserved) for Chapter 5 fig. 7, Chapter 7 fig. 8; *Daily Express* for Chapter 1 fig. 10, Chapter 7 fig. 5; *Daily Mirror* for Chapter 5 fig. 5; Esso Petroleum Co. Ltd. for Chapter 1 fig. 7, and Chapter 4 fig. 7; the Greater London Council for Chapter 9 figs. 6, 7 and 8, Chapter 10 figs. 5, 6, 7 and 9; GWR Museum for Chapter 4 fig. 2; John Hilleson Agency (copyright Berry-magnum) for Chapter 2 fig. 9; Keystone Press for Chapter 1 figs. 6, 8, 9, Chapter 2 figs. 4, 8, Chapter 4 fig. 8, Chapter 6 fig. 6, Chapter 8 fig. 7, Chapter 10 fig. 8; J. Lyon and Co. Ltd. for Chapter 8 fig. 5; Manchester Engineer and Surveyor's Department for Chapter 5 fig. 2; the Mansell Collection for Chapter 7 fig. 2, Chapter 8 fig. 1; Ministry of Agriculture, Food and Fisheries, for Chapter 3 figs. 5 and 7; National Coal Board for Chapter 2 figs. 1 and 2; National Film Archives for Chapter 11 fig. 7; Paul Popper Ltd. for Chapter 9 fig. 3, and 'Macmillan' on page 94; Publicity Presentations for Chapter 11 fig. 6; Radio Times Hulton Picture Library for Chapter 2 fig. 6, Chapter 3 figs. 1, 2, 3, Chapter 5 figs. 1, 6, 8, Chapter 6 figs. 2, 7, 8, Chapter 7 figs. 1, 3, 4, 6, Chapter 9 figs. 1, 9, 11, Chapter 10 figs. 2, 4, Chapter 11 fig. 5, all pictures on page 94 except 'Macmillan'; 'Shelter' for Chapter 7 fig. 10; Syndication International for Chapter 5 fig. 4, Chapter 11 figs. 1, 4, 8; *Times* Newspapers for Chapter 8 fig. 4; TUC for Chapter 8 fig. 3; UK Atomic Energy Authority for Chapter 6 fig. 3; Wilkinson Sword for Chapter 2 fig. 5. Chapter 1 fig. 5 is from *Assorted Sizes* by Osbert Lancaster and is reproduced by permission of the publisher John Murray.

Introduction

How do we know what life was really like in the past? How do the writers of history books find out? Well, if they are writing about ancient times they may have to rely partly on a study of ruins (such as at Stonehenge), of remains dug up by archaeologists (as at Sutton Hoo), of drawings made by cavemen or tools used by Bronze Age workmen. All these things are 'documents' which tell us something about the past.

If the historian is writing about more modern times he can use written or printed material such as the diaries of Samuel Pepys or the Reports of Royal Commissions into Factory Conditions in the nineteenth century. Nowadays many of these printed documents have been published so that they can be used by young history students. We no longer have to rely completely on the textbook for our ideas of what life was like in 1500 or 1700 or 1900; we can now read the original documents ourselves.

Most of these collections of documents consist of printed material. This is almost natural since history is, after all, a story and a story is best told in words. But some of these printed documents are very long, the language is often very difficult, so that many of us are unwilling to use them.

It is different with illustrated material; we have an example of the difference if we look at the beginning of the 'Shelter' campaign. There had been dozens of Blue Books and White Papers on the problems of housing in modern Britain; there had been many learned articles, as well as shorter articles in the popular newspapers. But it was only after the BBC had shown the play *Cathy Come Home* that the real plight of the homeless was brought home to people; on the day after the first showing of this film, Des Wilson and a group of young friends decided to do something and 'Shelter' was born. The visual evidence had made much more impact on them than had the written word.

The same is true of the social history of modern Britain. We can of course study it through the written document, but we may understand the problem of nineteenth-century poverty more clearly if we see a contemporary photograph of a group of barefooted children (Book 2, Chapter 9, Picture 8). Similarly, we can read about the problems of old age, but the photograph of the inmates of an Old People's Home in 1880 (Book 2, Chapter 7, Picture 6) brings out clearly what life was really like for these unfortunate people.

Of course the picture document, like the written document, has to be used very carefully by the historian. He has to ask questions about it, compare one picture with another, compare the evidence presented by the photograph with the evidence collected elsewhere—in the written word for example. It would be bad history, for instance, to conclude that all working-class people were very poor in 1900; yet this is certainly the evidence of some pictures (Book 2, Chapter 7, Picture 7). But these pictures do not tell the whole story because there were other working class people who were well off at this time (Book 2, Chapter 8, Picture 2). The job of the historian is to weigh up one piece of evidence with another before he begins to write his story.

In these three volumes I have tried to show how the historian works: there are questions about the pictures which will help to bring out the significance of the evidence presented; there are other questions which ask the Young Historian to compare one piece of evidence with another; there are questions which direct the Young Historian's attention to plays, novels or other written documents.

I have also tried to offer the Young Historian a variety of work—painting, letter-writing, reading—which will help him to recreate for himself, by his own imagination, what the past was like. These questions are not meant to be a final, complete list; there are many other questions to be asked on the pictures and many other kinds of work that might be tackled. The questions, like the picture-documents, are only illustrative and not exhaustive.

1 Living Standards 1914–70

My income and yours

In *David Copperfield*, Mr Micawber said: 'Annual income twenty pounds, annual expenditure nineteen pounds, nineteen and six—result happiness. Annual income twenty pounds, annual expenditure twenty pounds, ought and sixpence—result misery'. Each of us knows that Mr Micawber was right—we cannot spend more than we earn. Our personal income is one of the main factors which decides the standard of living at which we live—what kind of house, clothes, furniture and food we have, what holidays we enjoy, how we travel and spend our leisure time. If we have a small income we enjoy a lower standard of living than people who have a high income.

Our income is one factor which decides our living standards. Another factor is our own decision on how we spend that income. If we decide to save a good deal of our income then we will have a lower standard of living than if we had spent it all. Similarly, if we decide to spend a lot of money on clothes then we will have less to spend on holidays.

The nation's income

Every day the people of this country use their *labour* and, with the help of different kinds of machinery or equipment (or *capital*) they produce certain goods or provide certain services. In some cases this produce is easy to measure: we can go to a brickyard and count the number of bricks which the men have made in a day. In other cases it is difficult to measure accurately what a person has produced at the end of a day. How, for example, can we measure the output of a teacher or nurse?

1 In wartime some of the nation's wealth is destroyed and part of its national income is used up to provide munitions, clothes, transport and other things needed by the Services. In addition there is a smaller national income in wartime than in peacetime since men, such as these, who are involved in fighting, are not producing anything.

One way is to add up the incomes which people receive for the work they do, whether producing something like bricks or cars, or providing some service such as teachers, nurses, clerks and many others do. The total of their incomes is the *nation's income*—and is a measure of the goods and services provided by the nation.

Some nations have a high income—the USA in 1970 had an average income of about £800 per person (man, woman and child). In Britain the average is about £500. In India it is about £30. The main reason for the differences between these countries is the difference in their industrial development. America has gone further along the road of industrial progress: her workpeople produce more wealth each working hour than do the people of Britain—who in turn produce much more than do the people in India.

National income and living standards

The USA has a very high national income—and the people of the USA enjoy a very high standard of living. They have more cars, better roads, more university students, bigger newspapers and more varied food than the British have. Both the Americans and the British have more telephones, schoolteachers and holidays than the Indians can afford. As countries become more industrialised so the nation's income rises—and so does the standard of living of its inhabitants.

Dividing the nation's income

We have seen that the size of our personal income is only one factor in deciding our standard of living: another important factor is the decisions we make about the use of that income. In the same way the nation's total income is only one factor in deciding the nation's standard of living: another important factor is the answer given to the question: 'How is the national income to be divided up?' There are many ways in which we might spend part or indeed all of the income: we might spend more on defence or war, or build more offices, hospitals and schools, and fewer houses, bridges and factories. We might spend more on food and less on machinery, more on entertainment and less on education.

War and standards of living

During this period (1914–70) Britain took a leading part in two World Wars and after 1950 spent an increasingly large part of her national income on rearming, as part of the defence of the free world against the threat of a Communist attack. One immediate effect of war and rearming is to reduce the nation's standard of living: men who might have been producing goods or providing a service went into the armed forces and fought in the war (Picture 1). Material which might have been used to provide goods for use at home or for exports had to be used to make the guns and other munitions needed in the war.

However, for some people, the war led to a rise in the standard of living. Some of the soldiers had previously been unemployed: their service pay, and particularly the allowances paid by the government to their wives and children, meant

2 In the 1970s Britain is no longer 'the workshop of the world' as she had been in the middle of the nineteenth century. This graph shows that Britain's decline began in the nineteenth century.

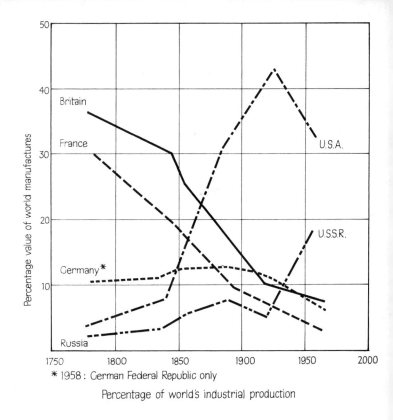

Percentage value of world manufactures

* 1958: German Federal Republic only

Percentage of world's industrial production

that some families had a higher income during the war. Many women went to work during the wars—either in farming (Chapter 3, Picture 1) or in the munitions industry. Their families enjoyed a higher income and standard of living during the war than in time of peace.

One lasting effect of the war was in the export trade. Britain was already facing strong foreign competition from Germany and the USA (Book 2, Chapter 1, Picture 9). During the First World War British exporters were unable to supply goods to foreign markets. Our former customers either went to the USA or Japan for their goods, or they learned to make them for themselves. In either case once the war was over British exporters found it even more difficult to sell their goods overseas.

Boom and depression 1919–39

When the First World War ended in 1918 there was a demand for goods—to rebuild industry, to satisfy the demands of the prosperous consumers. In 1919 and 1920 wages and profits were high as industry expanded. But once this immediate burst of activity had taken place there was the beginning of a slump in trade (Picture 2), employment and wages. Long term unemployment had been a feature of the late nineteenth century (Book 2, Chapter 2, Picture 7): it was to be a permanent feature of British life from 1921 until 1939 (Chapter 2, Picture 6: Chapter 7, Pictures 1 and 9). Many employers thought that the main reason for our failure to regain our export markets was that British wage rates were too high.

3 *(left)* Because timber, wool, cotton and other raw materials were very cheap during the depression of the 1920s and 1930s manufacturers were able to produce cars, furniture and other goods very cheaply. This was one reason why many people enjoyed a rise in their living standards during this period of depression; anyone with a regular job and a steady wage benefited from falling prices.

4 *(right)* The Second World War was the most destructive the world had ever seen; air raids on Britain's major cities and towns destroyed millions of homes, shops, factories, and port installations—all of which had to be replaced after the war. Part of the post-war national income had to be used to make good the damage done in wartime.

They tried to force the trade unions to accept wage cuts. But the workers had got used to a high standard of living in the immediate post-war years: they were unwilling to accept a smaller share in the national income. This was a major cause of the General Strike in 1926.

New industry and a high standard of living
During the 1930s there were always about two million men out of work and another three or four million who worked only part-time. However at the same time as the coal, cotton, shipbuilding and steel industries were suffering, there were new industries which were expanding. Some of these had started before 1914 (Book 2, Chapter 2). In the 1930s the car, aircraft, chemical, aluminium, rayon and other new industries expanded (Chapter 2, Pictures 3 and 4). In such industries men and employers were highly paid.

One of the reasons for the depression in British exports was that the food-growing countries (many of which were British colonies) were getting a low price for their products (Chapter 3, Picture 3). But low prices for their exports meant low prices for Britain's imports which were reflected in the price of clothes (Picture 3), of houses (Chapter 5, Picture 2) and the price of food (Chapter 8, Picture 6). For those who had a steady job and a steady wage or salary these falling prices meant a rise in living Standard—in the middle of a great depression and mass unemployment.

The Second World War and the nation's income

Between 1939 and 1945 millions of British homes were destroyed or damaged (Picture 4): so were factories, marshalling yards, ports, offices and so on. One effect of this was felt after the war: the rebuilding of these bomb-damaged properties meant that part of the nation's income had to be set aside to replace what had been destroyed: it did not add much that was new to the nation's wealth, it merely replaced what had been there before. During this war, as during the first, men went to serve in the forces (Picture 6) and material had to be used up to make munitions. This led to a long period of shortages (Picture 5) when

5 *(left)* There was a world-wide shortage of many materials in the years following the end of the war. Britain had to buy her share of these scarce goods on the international markets. Because of their high price and scarcity Britain could not afford to buy all that she wanted. This resulted in a shortage of many goods, which led to a system of rationing and licensing to ensure as fair a distribution as possible.

6 *(right)* The Forces Education Service organised lectures for members of the Services and among other things organised Mock Elections to prepare the men for the General Election. The results of these elections (including this one) help to explain why Bomber Harris, an Air Force Chief, was able to inform Churchill that '80% of the service vote will be a Labour vote'.

'Thaird floor: No crockery, no hardware, no toys, and precious little baby linen.'

7 The oil refinery at Fawley. The building of refineries such as this helped to create employment in post-war Britain.

people could not get petrol, clothes, food, fuel or household articles for the kitchen.

This period of shortage went on after 1945. The national income grew (Picture 11) as houses, factories, oil refineries, steelworks, schools and so on, were built. But there was little material left over for making the goods which the people wanted: and because of a rising imports bill many of these scarce goods had to be exported. The rebuilding of a new Britain (Picture 7) meant full employment and high wages. The government created a Welfare State which again meant employment for many thousands of people (Chapter 6, Pictures 5 and 6): welfare clinics and schools (Chapter 5, Picture 6 and Chapter 10, Pictures 7 and 8) meant employment for many thousands more. But all this cost money and material—an increasing part of the nation's income was set aside for rebuilding or for exports, and there was less for people in this country. Rationing continued to be a feature of British life until the 1950s (Chapter 6, Picture 4).

Affluence
By the middle of the 1950s Britain had built her new industries and established her Welfare State. The old and new industries were producing ever-increasing

8 The affluent society is reflected in the shops as well as in the shoppers.

9 Investors in the stock market have gained from the rise in British living standards. As people have more money to spend, manufacturers have been able to make large profits by selling an ever increasing volume of goods. These profits explain the rise in the prices of so many shares.

10 Rising prices have led to balance of payments problem as British exports become too dear while foreign importers have been encouraged to try to sell their goods in the British market. One solution to this problem is devaluation which Britain tried in 1949 and 1967.

11 The national income shows an almost continued growth; part of this growth is due to rising prices, but part of it is due to a real increase in output—and so a real increase in living standards.

GROWTH OF NATIONAL INCOME

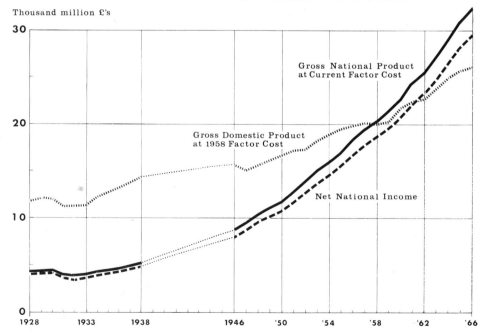

amounts of goods. Now, in the 1950s, there was less need to set aside so much for rebuilding: more could be set free for consumption at home. The high profits made in industry (Picture 9) and the high wages paid to a fully employed work-people could be spent on British and foreign goods. By 1960 Britain was enjoying a very high standard of living (Picture 8).

Inflation

One effect of full employment is that employers are forced to pay high wages to attract workmen to their factories or to keep those they already have. This leads to firms putting up their prices—to get back some of the increased wages bill. When British goods get more expensive some of our overseas customers stop buying them. In order to avoid this the British government has twice been forced to devalue the pound—once in 1949 and again in 1967. Devaluation means that British exporters find it easier to sell although British imports cost more. Thus: if we assume that a British car costs £1,000 in 1948 when £ = 4·03, the car sold in USA for \$4030; after devaluation in 1949 when £ = 2·80 the car sold in USA for \$2800; and after £ was devalued in 1967 when £ = 2·40 the car sold in USA for \$2400.

National income and social change

In 1972 the mass of the British people enjoy a very high standard of living. Because of Britain's industrial output we have been able to build millions of new houses, new schools and welfare clinics, motorways and factories, shopping centres and office blocks. Millions of families now have two or three wage-earners because many mothers go to work. High wages and constant employment have allowed millions to buy a high standard of living for themselves.

The Young Historian

1. Picture 1 shows men in the trenches during the war. You can see some of these men at the recruiting office in Chapter 6, Picture 8. Can you suggest three jobs which some of these men might have been doing in peacetime? Why does the national income go down during wartime? (See also Picture 4 and Chapter 7, Picture 5).
2. Picture 2 shows how Britain's share of world trade declined. How does this help to explain the unemployment in the depressed areas of Britain (Chapter 2, Picture 6 and Chapter 7, Pictures 1 and 5).
3. Why was there more destruction of property in the Second than in the First World War? Perhaps your town was one of those which was damaged during the Second War. Find out the names of three cities which were badly damaged.

Why did such damage result in a smaller share of the nation's income being available for consumers after 1945? (Picture 4, and Chapter 6, Picture 5).

4. Picture 6 shows that British soldiers voted in a mock election in 1944. Find out the result of the first post-war General Election in 1945. Who was the first Labour Prime Minister? Why were some people surprised at this result?

5. Where is Fawley (Picture 7)? Why does modern Britain need an increased quantity of petrol and other fuels? (See also Chapter 4). How does a refinery like this add to the national income?

6. How did the growth in the national income (Picture 11) explain the end of shortages (Picture 5) and the coming of the affluent society (Picture 8)?

7. Write a letter from home to a soldier at the Front explaining why you want to war to end. (Pictures 1, 2, 5 and 6).

8. Paint or draw your own version of either (i) Britain at war or (ii) the affluent society.

2 Industry

British industry 1914

In Book 2, Chapter 2, we saw that at the end of the nineteenth century there were a number of new technological developments which led to the establishment of new industries—such as the chemical industry (Book 2, Chapter 2, Picture 4) and the electrical engineering industries (Book 2, Chapter 2, Picture 5). We also saw that Germany and the USA had been quick to take up these new industries (Book 2, Chapter 1, Picture 9) and that they had captured a large part of world trade by 1914. British industrialists were slow to invest in these new industries: they preferred to rely on the old British industries of cotton, coal, steel and shipbuilding.

Post-war industry

After 1918 all of these old industries went through a long period of depression. British coal mines were not as mechanised as those of Germany, Poland or the USA (Picture 1) so that output costs were high and overseas customers refused to buy British coal. There was anyhow a fall in the demand for coal as shipping lines began to use oil as a fuel and modern factories used electricity instead of steam power. Cotton suffered from Japanese and Indian competition as well as from the development of man-made fibres such as rayon. As the price of textiles fell (Chapter 1, Picture 3), so British firms were forced to close down. Britain had been the world's leading shipbuilder in 1900: by 1918 there were other countries competing with Britain in this field—and there was a fall in the world demand for ships after 1921.

1 The physical hardship and danger of working in an old coal mine is illustrated in this picture. The output from such a mine depends to a large extent on physical strength and not on mechanical aids.

2 In the mechanised pits the output depends less on physical strength since the machines do so much of the work. This means that fewer miners are needed to produce the required volume of coal. In the short term this leads to unemployment in the mining districts; in the long term the nation benefits, as the ex-miners are trained to produce something else which can be added to the national income. (Chapter 7, Picture 8.)

Depressed areas

Coal, cotton, shipbuilding and steel went through a period of depression: factories, mines, works and yards closed down as employers were unable to sell their products. Men went to Labour Exchanges in search of work (Picture 6 and Chapter 7, Pictures 1 and 9). Throughout the 1920s there were never less than $1\frac{1}{2}$ million men out of work: in the 1930s the number rose to over 3 million (Chapter 7, Picture 9). But the graphs do not tell the whole story: this unemployment was heaviest in certain parts of the country—in Jarrow two men out of three were out of work when a shipyard closed down: in Merthyr and Dowlais over half the men were unemployed when three steel works closed: in some mining valleys of Wales and mining villages of Scotland nearly all the men were out of work.

At the same time there were areas which suffered little unemployment. In the Midlands and the South East the development of the car industry (Picture 3)

3 An assembly line in which machinery does a good deal of the work and helps to make the worker more productive. This allows the employer to offer higher wages.

4 Working on Concorde. Modern industries, such as aircraft building, depend on the skills of a variety of workpeople—from designers to fitters. The addition made to the national income by the work of these men is much greater than the addition made by a miner in an old-fashioned pit (Picture 1). The progressive country is the one which has more of the modern industries and less of the old-fashioned, physical-strength industries.

provided employment for millions: in these areas, too, were the firms producing rayon, aluminium and the new manufactured foods. People in Luton and Oxford, Coventry and Birmingham, London suburbs, saw very little unemployment. For them, with their steady incomes, life was good—with its falling prices for houses, clothes and food, they enjoyed a rising standard of living. Many of them bought houses, cars, furniture and holidays, for the first time.

Industry and the Second World War

One effect of the Second World War was the development of many new industrial techniques. In particular, there was a series of developments in the aircraft industry: in 1939 there was no engine strong enough to drive passenger aircraft across the Atlantic to the USA. By 1945 such flights were commonplace and the development of the jet engine by Frank Whittle suggested a continuation of advancement in aircraft design. This led to a new industry (Picture 4) which, in 1972 employs many thousands of highly skilled and highly paid workers.

There were developments in the petro-chemicals industry which led to the growth of firms such as ICI producing paints and medicine, nylon and explosives, and employing thousands of people. The growth of the car industry led to a growth in the demand for petrol—and so to the building of a number of gigantic oil refineries (Chapter 1, Picture 7) where highly-qualified people work.

5   Workers in Wilkinson Sword's modern, automated factory where skills are valuable and conditions are pleasant.

6   A dole queue—a common feature of life in the depressed period between the wars (1919–39) and, unfortunately, a feature of life in the depressed areas of Britain since 1945. Unemployed workers contribute nothing towards the national income; the job of the government is to help create work for such people so that they can make a meaningful contribution and so raise the nation's living standards.

7 Since the Second World War many new factories have been built in trading estates like this one.

In some of the old industries there were attempts to catch up with the past: the coal industry became more mechanised (Picture 2): employers invested in modern machinery so getting an increased output per workman employed.

One effect of this modernisation process was to increase the demand for highly skilled workpeople—to design the machines as well as to maintain them. This in turn has led to a massive increase in the amount of money spent by the government on education (Chapter 10) so that in 1972 many thousands of boys and girls go on to some form of training when they leave school. .

New industry and the national income

When Britain decided to rebuilt her bomb-damaged towns and to mechanise her pits, to modernise her railways and to build oil refineries (Chapter 1, Picture 7), a large part of the national income had to be set aside for such building. When the government decided to build new towns (Chapter 5, Picture 9) and rehouse the slum dwellers (Chapter 5, Picture 7), as well as to build schools and welfare clinics (Chapter 5, Picture 6) another part of the nation's income had to set aside. This meant that there was less of that income for people to enjoy in the shape of goods in the shops, thus bringing about a period of shortage (Chapter 1, Picture 5) and rationing (Chapter 6, Picture 4).

However, once new industries are built and old industries modernised, there is an increased output from both new and old—and the national income grows rapidly (Chapter 1, Picture 11). Once these industries have been developed a

23

8 A rich country, such as Britain has been since 1950, can afford to devote part of its labour force and its other resources to providing its people with luxury services—such as hairdressing illustrated here. In poorer countries such luxuries are rarer.

9 A view of South Wales, a reminder of the grim industrial past and its effects on the environment. This was part of the price paid for industrial development and national enrichment.

higher share of a higher national income is available in the shape of goods in the shops. The highly-paid workers and their employers can afford to pay for these goods—so that homes are better furnished (Chapter 9, Picture 3), more people own cars (Chapter 4 Picture 4) and enjoy more leisure time (Chapter 11). They can afford to pay for more and more services—so that more records are made and sold, more restaurants and cafés open and every High Street has its hairdressing salon (Picture 8).

Two nations?
In London and the Midlands, parts of South Wales and the South East, the majority of the people enjoy a high standard of living in what is now called the affluent society. However, in other parts of the country life is grimmer: in the coal towns and villages, in areas which still depend on the older industries there is still high unemployment and low wages. There are less job opportunities for working mothers and for school leavers. In such areas there is a lower standard of living than is enjoyed in the more prosperous parts of the country. South Wales is one such area (Picture 9).

The Young Historian

1. Look at Pictures 1 and 2. Write a letter from a man working in the old mine to one working in the new, in which he talks about their different conditions.
2. Why is there less need for physical strength in modern, mechanised industries than in the older industries? (See Pictures 1, 2 and 3).
3. Why does the modern firm have to spend more money on machinery and equipment than older firms had to? (See Pictures 2, 3, 4 and 5).
4. Why do workpeople in modern industries (Picture 5) need more education than people in the older industries? (Picture 1). Suggest three ways in which post-1945 governments have tried to do something about this.
5. Look at Picture 6. Why are these men queueing up? What do they hope to get? Why were there more of these queues in South Wales than in the South East of England?
6. Hairdressing (Picture 8) is a service industry, giving a service rather than producing an article or product. Find out the names of three other service industries. Why are such industries more common in modern industrialised societies than in primitive societies?
7. The poet Blake wrote about Dark Satanic Mills when describing the nineteenth century textile industry (See Picture 9). Why are modern industries less dirty?

3 Agriculture

Farming 1914-18

In Book 2, Chapter 3 we saw that by the end of the nineteenth century many British farmers had been ruined by the huge imports of cheap food from America, Argentina and Australasia. During the war more food had to be grown in the country because there was not enough shipping available to bring in all that was needed—the ships had to carry war material and troops. Since many of the men had volunteered for the armed forces (Chapter 1, Picture 1 and Chapter 6, Picture 8), the extra labour required had to be provided by women (Picture 1), or in some cases by boys (Picture 2). When the Germans launched a very successful submarine campaign against ships coming to Britain—in 1917—the country was saved from starvation by the output of British farmers helped by unskilled workers such as these.

Depression 1919-39

Once the war was over the world returned to a more normal pattern of trade: Britain had a policy of Free Trade which allowed the import of any article into

1   Women at work on farms during the First World War (1914-18). Many farmworkers entered the fighting services (Chapter 1, Picture 1) and women who demanded 'the right to serve' took their place.

2 Boys from Eton School working on a farm in wartime.

the country without any import duties. This meant that once again overseas farmers sent their wheat, meat, dairy produce and so on, to Britain, at prices which the British farmer could not compete with (Picture 3). Overseas farmers expanded their output, used more and more mechanised methods of farming—and so drove down the price of their product. In the long run this meant that they too faced hardship: the Australian wool farmer, for instance, saw the price of his wool tumble—but he had no alternative but to go on farming, or face starvation. As his income fell he bought fewer goods in the Australian shops, and so British exports to Australia declined. The cheap prices earned by overseas farmers is one of the reasons for the fall in British trade (Chapter 1, Picture 2).

However, these cheap prices were of great benefit to those people who had a job. They saw the price of clothing (Chapter 1, Picture 3) and of housing (Chapter 5, Picture 2) and of motor cars (Chapter 4) fall—because the price of the imported raw materials used in these products was falling. This meant that many millions of people enjoyed a rising standard of living—although many millions were unemployed because of these same falling prices.

3 A graph illustrating the fall in prices 1919–39. This fall in world prices for food and raw materials affected the incomes of people in many foreign countries (Australia, New Zealand and so on) who could then buy less from Britain. This was one of the causes of the heavy unemployment suffered in Britain in this period. But falling prices also led to low prices in the shops (Chapter 1, Picture 3) from which many people benefited.

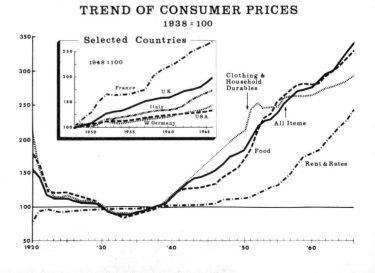

TREND OF CONSUMER PRICES
1938 = 100

4 Women at work on farms during the Second World War (1939–45).

Government aid to farming—1930–39

British governments seemed to be overwhelmed by the size of their problems in the 1930s. They made little effort to help people in the depressed areas of South Wales and the North East; not until 1932 did they give up the policy of Free Trade —although they still allowed the free importing of food from countries in the British Empire. They set up a number of Boards to help some farmers, e.g. the Milk Marketing Board tried to help dairy farmers. Sugar beet farmers were helped by a system of subsidies, which encouraged the growth of sugar beet to replace the imported sugar and so help the Balance of Payments.

The Second World War

Between 1939 and 1945 British farmers again saved the country from starvation. Since the war was even bigger than the First World War—more countries were involved and the destruction was greater—there was even less chance of importing foreign food into this country. While the government limited what people could buy—by a system of rationing (Chapter 6, Picture 4)—it also encouraged British farmers to increase their output to provide the food that was needed. Once again women were persuaded to work on the land (Picture 4) as in 1914.

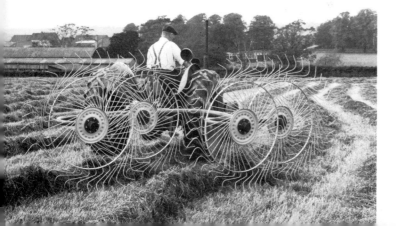

5 Modern farm machinery, such as this, helps to make each worker much more productive than his unaided predecessor. This means that each worker contributes more to the national income.

6 Haymaking on a farm, 1924. Some farms are still unmechanised and so are less productive than they might be. But mechanisation costs money which owners of small farms in particular may not be able to afford.

Aid to farmers 1945–70

Since 1945 Britain has had to import an increasing amount of raw material and machinery—to build the houses (Chapter 5, Picture 7), steelworks (Chapter 6, Picture 5), refineries (Chapter 1, Picture 7), that a modern country needs. At the same time British exporters have had to try to sell more abroad to earn the money needed to pay for these increased imports. Between 1945 and 1955 there was a great need for a huge increase in imports—to help the country to recover from the effects of the war. During this time it was difficult to increase exports at the same rate. The government therefore tried to cut down on imports—by continuing the system of rationing. They saw that if British farmers continued to provide a large part of the food required in this country this would mean that less would need to be imported—and so the Balance of Payments would be helped.

The first post-war Agriculture Act was passed in 1947 and its ideas have been followed by all post-war governments. The Act said that every year the government would fix the prices to be received by the farmer for his eggs, milk, wheat and so on. This meant that the farmer would be guaranteed a certain income—and since the National Farmers Union helps to fix the level of these prices, the farmer could expect to get a good bargain. The government did not stop the free importing of cheap food from abroad—this would have hurt British exporters. So we have a system under which, for example, butter is imported, sold on the market for—say—20p per lb. while the government guarantees that the British farmer will get—say—$22\frac{1}{2}$p per lb. for his butter. The housewife gains from cheap

7 A mechanised farm.

food: the farmer gains from a guaranteed income—made up partly of the 20p he received from the market and the $2\frac{1}{2}$p per lb. he receives from the government. This system of guaranteed prices and subsidies has helped British farmers to buy the machinery they need to become more efficient (Picture 5). With modern machinery the farmer needs fewer workpeople (Pictures 6 and 7) so that the output per workman is greater. This has allowed the farmer to pay better wages to his workers so that the standard of living has gone up.

Factory Farming
During the 1960s British farmers learned about new methods—of feeding cattle, of rearing pigs, of egg-producing. Many of these new methods involve a large outlay on new buildings (Picture 7), in some of which chickens, lambs, calves and other animals are kept, and fed in a scientific way so that the output is greater than it would have been if the animals had been left free to roam the fields. Some people oppose this factory farming: they think that it is cruel to the animals and that the food produced is less tasty than that produced by natural farming. However, many millions now enjoy cheap food, and a more varied diet, so that their health has improved (Chapter 5, Picture 10). There are still hundreds of small farms where

there is very little machinery but such farms are finding it increasingly difficult to compete with the mechanised, modernised farm.

Agriculture and the national income

A prosperous agricultural industry supplies about half the food we eat, at cheap prices. This is a help to our Balance of Payments—if farmers did not produce this then we would either have to be exporting more goods or we would have to cut down on the imports of other things in order to pay for the food we would need to import. Mechanised farms are adding to the national income while at the same time they are releasing thousands of men and women from working on the farms. They are then available for work elsewhere, so further adding to the national income.

The Young Historian

1. Why was there a need for more home-grown food during the First and Second World Wars? How did this affect (i) the incomes of British farmers (ii) the British national income?

2. Look at Pictures 1 and 2 again. Why was war work done by boys and women? (See also Chapter 1, Picture 1). How did this affect the family-income of the women's families?

3. Look at Picture 3. What sort of things does Britain import? How does this graph help to explain (i) cheap clothes available in Britain in the 1930s (Chapter 1, Picture 3), (ii) a falling in price of houses in the 1930s (Chapter 5, Picture 2), and (iii) cheap food in Britain in the 1930s (Chapter 8, Picture 6)? Can you say who gained from these falling prices?

4. Which countries suffered when prices fell? Write a letter from one of these countries explaining why you can't buy a new British car or new British clothes. Which British industries suffered from this fall in British exports in the 1930s?

5. Why are there fewer farmworkers in the 1960s than in the 1920s? What does this tell you about the amount of wealth produced by each farmworker in the 1960s? Can you suggest where the other workers have gone?

6. Draw or paint haymaking in 1920 or in 1960. Which haymaking produced the most fun for the children of the village?

7. Modern industrialists have to have a lot of money (Chapter 1, Picture 7). Is this true of the modern farmers? Why?

8. Why is the smaller farmer unable to buy the latest machinery? What effect does this have on the amount produced by each of his workmen?

4 Transport

The internal combustion engine

In Book 2, Chapter 4, we saw that by 1914 there were a number of petrol-driven cars on the British roads but that the main method of town transport was the horse and the electric tram, and the main method of inter-city transport was the railway train.

This period (1914–70) has seen a revolution in land transport which has changed the life of the people in the same way as the invention of the railway did. Lorries carrying goods to and from factories and to and from shopping centres have allowed factory owners to build their factories away from the railway yards. They have allowed the growth of shopping centres which can be supplied with goods carried on these lorries. The development of the bus (Picture 2) revolutionised travel into and inside our towns. People could come in from country villages to shop or go to the cinema or football games; men could go to work, their wives go shopping, their children go to school—cheaply.

1 *(left)* Early motor cars were modelled on the existing horse-drawn carriages. They were hand-built, expensive luxuries for the very rich.

2 *(right)* An early petrol-driven omnibus which soon replaced the horse-drawn omnibus but had a quieter rival, the electric tram.

Above all, the privately-owned motor car has allowed a freedom of movement to whole families which has altered their pattern of living. People travel to work (Picture 3), go for outings at weekends and during their holidays (Chapter 11, Picture 3) in a way that was unthinkable in 1914. As more and more people earn higher wages (Chapter 7, Picture 7), so they are able to spend more on leisure and entertainment—and one of their first 'buys' is a motor car. In the 1920s and 1930s this was the privilege of the middle classes, who copied the habits of their aristocratic social superiors (Book 2, Chapter 4): since 1950 the number of privately-owned cars has increased so that by 1972 over half the households in the country has a car and nearly one in ten has two cars.

The railways

As the volume of goods carried by road increased so there was a decline in the volume carried by rail. Similarly, if more people travel by road, less travel by rail. During the 1930s few of the railway companies made any profits; during the war the railway system suffered from bombing, while there was little or no chance of replacing old and worn out engines and rolling stock. The railway system is essential to industrial Britain; not even the new motorways could carry all the goods used in a modern society. But the companies earning little, if any, profit could not afford to modernise the system. So, in 1947, the government nationalised the railways and spent many millions of pounds replacing the old engines and building modern, electrified lines. Many lines have been closed because they were losing too much money but by 1970 there were signs that the modernised railway system had begun to recapture some of the freight and passengers lost to the roads and to air travel.

Transport and Employment

The development of the petrol engine and of the new railway system have been major factors in creating jobs for millions of people. There are those who have to build the engines or motor cars (Chapter 2, Picture 3), and aircraft (Chapter 2, Picture 4): there are those who have to build the new lines and motorways (Picture 4); there are the millions working in the engineering and oil industries (Chapter 1, Picture 7), as well as in the garages and ships which distribute the petrol (Picture 7).

There are insurance companies which deal with car insurance, traffic wardens, as well as civil servants at the Ministry of Transport—all of whom are employed because of the development of new methods of transport.

Air travel

In 1914 the airplane was in its infancy (Book 2, Chapter 4), although some aircraft were used during the First World War. Between 1919 and 1939 a number of improvements were made; engines became more reliable and stronger; aircraft frames were bigger and sturdier. But even so the Hannibal, (Picture 5), which ran

3 *(left)* In our more affluent society millions of people can afford the cheaper mass-produced cars.

4 *(right)* The building of motorways is the twentieth-century counterpart to the nineteenth-century's building of railways. One major difference is that the railways were built for private railway companies whereas the motorways are built for public authorities, and are paid for out of taxes and rates.

34

5 The aeroplane was a relatively slow machine of limited value until the technological developments which took place during the Second World War (1939–45).

on the Imperial routes never went at more than 100 mph, carrying eighteen passengers. There was no regular flight across the Atlantic to the USA.

The Second World War revolutionised air transport. Planes were built to carry hundreds of men, and bulky materials such as tanks; engines were designed to drive these larger aircraft; communications systems between the ground and the aircraft were improved—all so that a war might be won. In 1930 Frank Whittle had designed the first jet engine; in May 1941 the Gloster E28 achieved a speed of 370 mph, using his engine. By the end of the war both the British Gloster Meteor and the German ME 262 were using jet engines.

Since the war the aircraft companies have continued to build bigger, faster and safer aircraft (Picture 6) and the Concorde (Chapter 2, Picture 4) may soon be flying on the world's air routes at speeds up to 1,400 mph. Already Jumbo Jets carry 500 or more passengers on each trip, crossing the Atlantic in about four hours. These new aircraft are bought by airline companies (such as BEA and BOAC) which operate scheduled flights to almost every part of the world. The increase in the number of people travelling by air has meant the building of new

6 The modern aeroplane which allows people to travel across the world quickly, cheaply and safely.

7 A modern oil tanker. The increasing use of the petrol engine and the development of the petro-chemical industry have led to increased demands for oil. In the modern tanker a crew of perhaps 30 or 40 men run a ship of 300,000 tons or more. Their productivity is much greater than that of their predecessors in smaller ships.

and larger airports, in which hundreds of people are employed to help passengers and planes on their way.

Sea transport

In 1914 most of the world's ships were coal-burning vessels, although the British Navy had already gone over to oil-fired engines. Since 1914 an increasing number of ships have given up using coal—which helps to explain unemployment in the coal-producing areas of Britain. In 1914 Britain built about one half of the world's ships; since then Germany, the USA, Japan and Greece have built more efficient shipyards so that in 1970 Britain is only fifth in the table of shipbuilding countries. This again helps to explain unemployment in the shipbuilding areas of Scotland and the North East.

In 1919 the world had more ships than could profitably be used so that many merchant sailors were unemployed along with their shipbuilding colleagues. As one way of trying to provide employment, the government financed the building of the Queen Mary which was launched in 1935 and which proved to be the fastest

8 The Hovercraft was at first used for travel over water but the idea has been developed and in the near future we may be travelling on hovertrains.

liner. On such liners businessmen crossed the Atlantic, well-to-do people went on holiday cruises and many people emigrated in search of employment overseas.

The world's shipping lines suffered when the post-war revolution in air travel took place. Although merchant ships were still required—to carry the increasing quantity of goods into and out of the country—there was less demand for passenger vessels. People preferred to travel by air. In place of the large ocean liners the post-war world has seen the emergence of the gigantic oil tanker (Picture 7): already there are tankers of 100,000 tons dead weight and tankers of 350,000 tons are being built. These are required to carry the oil needed by the motoring public (Picture 3) and by the new petro-chemical industry (Chapter 1, Picture 7).

Britain can claim one modern development in sea transport. The Hovercraft (Picture 8) was invented by Christopher Cockerell and already there are regular passenger services across the Channel to France.

The Young Historian

1. Look at Picture 2. Write a story about 'Our first trip to the countryside'. Many city children only saw the countryside when they were evacuated during the war. Why didn't they go on outings such as these, in the 1930s?
2. Look at Picture 3. How does this help to illustrate (i) the affluence of modern Britain, (ii) the need for larger oil tankers (Picture 7) and more oil refineries (Chapter 1, Picture 7)?
3. Look at Picture 4. How far away from your town is the nearest Motorway? Find out who pays for the building of the Motorways. Why can such roads be built only in a developed society?
4. Look at Pictures 5 and 6. Write a letter from a pilot of an old airplane to one of the pilots in the new planes. Which one would you prefer to be?
5. The old airplanes were used by men and women who tried to show that flying to America or Australia was possible. Find out more about the work of Jim and Amy Mollison and of Amelia Erhardt.
6. Look at Picture 7. There are only forty crew on a ship carrying 100,000 tons of oil. What does this tell you about the amount of wealth produced by each sailor on a journey? Why can modern shipowners pay their sailors more than shipowners did in the 1930s?
7. How has the development of the petrol engine (Pictures 1, 2, 3 and 4), affected country life? (Think first of townspeople going into the countryside and then of the countryside people who benefit from the petrol engine.)
8. Draw or paint a train; a family outing in a car; a Youth Club or Church outing.

5 Health and Housing

War and housing and health

In Book 2, Chapter 5, we saw that by 1914 the government had passed a series of laws concerning housing; houses built after 1851 had to have a water supply laid on. Acts passed in the 1860s and 1870 had given local councils powers to pull down slum property and to build council houses in their place. The first Town and Country Planning Act had been passed in 1908 and some councils had already been influenced by the ideas of people like Ebenezer Howard who helped develop Welwyn Garden City.

During the war there was little new housebuilding so that many millions continued to live in the older parts of the industrial towns and cities where disease flourished in the overcrowded, insanitary slums. Many families had a higher income—as the women found work (Chapter 3, Picture 1) and their soldier fathers sent home a regular allowance; for many, the standard of living rose during the war—children had shoes, better food, as their parents had more money. But their housing standards remained very poor.

Throughout the war the government extended its powers in many ways—by 1918 industrialists were being told what they were to produce and their supplies

1 *(left)* The suburbs to which the middle class escaped from the towns; cheap methods of speedy travel were an essential requisite for such a move.

2 *(right)* Council houses built in the inter-war period, 1919–39. Although not enough was done in this period of cheap materials and mass unemployment, millions of people were provided with good housing and a chance to lead a different sort of life from that led by slum dwellers.

3 One of the less fortunate aspects of town development in the 1930s was strip-, or ribbon-building. It seemed as if every private house had to be built facing one of the new main roads built to carry the new motor cars.

of raw materials were controlled by a government department; food rationing meant an extension of government activity while the benefits of the National Insurance Acts were extended, first to the serving soldiers, then to workers in the munitions industries—adding to the number of civil servants and extending the power of the government. Once the war was over some people (including the civil servants) began to ask whether the government should not be as active in the war against poverty and disease as it had been in the war against Germany.

To try to win the war the government had been forced to appeal to people—to volunteer, to work hard, and so on; many politicians realised that such appeals coming from the better-off classes would have more chance of success if the less well-off believed that they were fighting for a better life for themselves. This led the politicians to promise that, once the war had been won, the country would have a better life in a land 'fit for heroes'.

Housing 1919–39
One of the first post-war Acts was the Housing Act (1919) which allowed councils to build houses for letting to the working classes; the government promised to give the councils a subsidy for each house that they built—which would lower the cost

4 Sir William Beveridge. He became one of the best known people in the country and his Report was a best seller; he can rightly claim to be one of the architects of the modern Welfare State which has helped to raise people's living standards.

of the house for the council and so allow it to offer the house at a lower rent than would otherwise be possible. Other similar Acts were passed in 1923, 1930 and 1934, and by 1939 over 1½ million council houses had been built (Picture 2). Many of these council estates sprung up on the outskirts of our industrial towns and cities; unfortunately, the rents were still too high for very many—who were unemployed (Chapter 7, Picture 9), and had no income other than the dole (Chapter 2, Picture 6). However, for those who were fortunate enough to get one of these houses, life was transformed. Out of the old, slum property (Chapter 7, Picture 2) they went into a new life—with gardens, airy, light rooms a good water supply and sometimes a bathroom. They enjoyed the same sort of privileges as the middle class suburbanites (Picture 1) although at a slightly different level. The growth of cheap and frequent bus services (Chapter 4), meant that they could afford to live away from their place of work and entertainment. The increasing number of lorries supplied the shops on these estates with goods bought by these prosperous working classes.

Private building 1919–39

The government helped the councils to build about $1\frac{1}{2}$ million new homes between 1919 and 1939. At the same time there were over $2\frac{1}{2}$ million new houses built for sale or rent by private builders. These houses (Picture 3) were cheap because there was a fall in the price of raw materials (Chapter 3, Picture 3) needed in these homes and because the wage rates were low since there were plenty of men anxious to get any sort of job. The increasing use of the motor car allowed many middle-class people to live in these suburban houses, travelling to work and entertainment in their cars. To help them to do so many private builders developed estates alongside existing main roads so that 'ribbon' or 'strip' building took place along miles of roads leading out of our towns.

Housing 1945–70

There was little, if any, housebuilding during the Second World War while, at the same time, there was the destruction of about three million homes. After the war the country had to be rebuilt—new industries had to be encouraged as well as old ones modernised which meant that a lot of raw material and machinery had to be imported. Thus there was less chance of importing everything else that we needed—so that food had to be rationed (Chapter 6, Picture 4), and the country went short of many things it would have liked to have had (Chapter 1, Picture 5). Among other things that had to wait was housing. Between 1945 and 1951 one million new houses were built—more than were built in any other European country but far less than was required by the people.

However, there still remain the old, decaying centres of our industrial cities and towns (Picture 8); each year about 100,000 old houses become unfit for habitation although people have to continue to live in them as there are not enough houses to go round. Campaigns such as that organised by 'Shelter' have brought this clearly before the public.

Health 1919–70

In the period 1919–39 the government extended the scope of the Health Service started by Lloyd George (Book 2, Chapter 5). More attention was paid to nursing mothers and a large number of child welfare clinics were opened (Picture 6). But in 1939 there were millions of people who never went to the doctor, could not afford necessary medicine, spectacles or dental treatment—all of which had to be paid for by the patient. In 1942 Sir William Beveridge (Picture 4) presented his report on Social Welfare in which he suggested that a free, universal National Health Service should be introduced as soon as possible. The Labour Party won the 1945 Election (Chapter 1, Picture 6) and by July 1948 Britain had its Health Service under which no one had to pay when being treated by the doctor, dentists or optician, or when getting medicine or hospital treatment. The cost of this Service was borne partly by the worker who paid a weekly contribution out of his wages, and mainly out of taxes collected by the Treasury. In 1951 the government

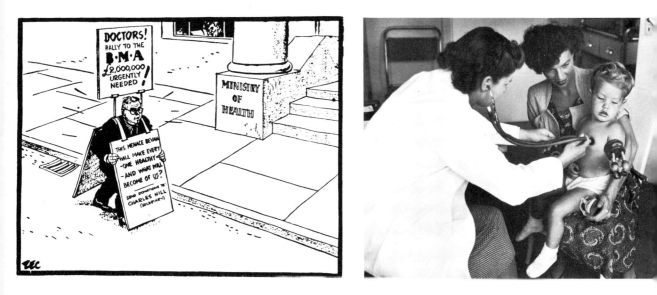

5 *(left)* Not everyone agreed with the introduction of the free Health Service. As in 1911 the major opposition to this service came from the doctors.

6 *(right)* A post-war welfare clinic where expectant mothers and young children receive medical attention. Only rich countries can afford such luxuries.

7 *(left)* A new housing estate, Park Hill Flats, Sheffield, which replaced nineteenth-century industrial slums. Not everyone is happy with this sort of development; many people miss the friendliness of the 'back-to-back' housing which they left behind.

8 *(right)* Too many people live in housing such as this. Here in Liverpool as in other large industrial cities and towns the relics of the nineteenth century still remain, and government and local authorities shy away from the huge cost of pulling down all the unfit houses and replacing them with modern, adequate estates.

9 One of the better features of post-war development has been the creation of a number of New Towns, one of which is Crawley (*above*). In these New Towns there is an air of affluence which leads some of the inhabitants to believe that 'there are no poor now'.

decided that patients should be asked to pay for part of their treatment; a prescription charge was introduced, as well as part payment for dental and optical treatment. Since then these charges have been increased, and since 1970 patients are expected to pay about half the cost of their medicine or dental treatment.

Effects of improved services

Since 1919 there have been major discoveries—such as penicillin and other drugs —as well as major medical advances in surgery. More and better trained doctors and nurses, using better equipment and medicines, have been able to work in modern clinics and hospitals to help fight disease and cure the sick. As people have

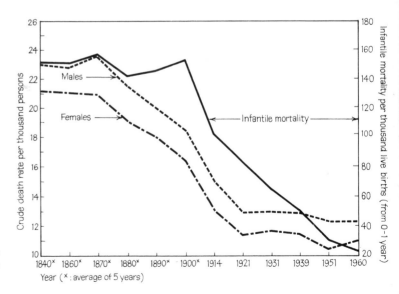

10 One of the results of better housing and a better diet has been a fall in mortality rates. New drugs and an improved health service have also played their part in reducing these rates.

moved into better houses and been able to afford better clothes and food so their health has improved. The falling mortality rates (Picture 10) are a reflection of a higher standard of living for the majority of the people—due to the continual development of technology and industry which makes this improvement possible.

The Young Historian

1. Look at Picture 1. What class of people lived in these suburbs? How were they affected by the fall in prices? (Chapter 3, Picture 3).
2. Find out how a building society helps people to buy houses. Houses were cheap in the 1930s (about £500). Work out the weekly cost of buying such a house when (i) the interest was three per cent and the money had to be repayed over twenty years, and (ii) the interest was eight per cent and the money had to be repayed over ten years.
3. Look at Picture 3. The first real attempts at providing council houses began in 1919. Write a letter to a relative explaining the differences between life in the old house, and in the new one.
4. Look at Picture 4. Beveridge wrote and spoke about five Giant Evils: Ignorance, Squalor, Disease, Poverty and Idleness. Write five paragraphs showing how governments have tackled each of these evils since 1945. Have they been completely eliminated?
6. Look at infant mortality rates, Picture 10. How many children per 1,000 died in (i) 1930 and (ii) 1960? Can you suggest three reasons for this fall? (Pictures 2 and 6; Chapter 3, Picture 3 (prices) and Chapter 9, Picture 4 (size of family).
7. Crawley New Town (Picture 9) is one of the towns built as a result of the New Towns Act of 1947. Find out the names of three other new towns. Compare life in such a town with life in: (i) Liverpool—Picture 8 (ii) suburban council houses—Picture 2.
8. Paint or draw your own versions of: (i) old housing; (ii) new housing.

6 Government—National and Local

By 1914 the British people had created a structure of national and local government to deal with the problems created by the continuing industrial revolution. Local government had been reformed in 1835, strengthened in 1871 and 1886, and given increased powers to deal with health and housing in many Acts passed in the 1860s and 1870s. In 1902 the local councils were given control of State education, largely because of the influence of Robert Morant—one of the first of the new civil servants, (Book 2, Chapter 6).

The structure of government has remained largely unaltered since 1914, although in 1929 the Boards of Guardians were abolished and their work taken over by local councils while, as the scope of government activity widened, so the number of civil servants has increased (Picture 1). But the basic structure of government remains what it was in 1914. We have been promised a major reform in this structure as a result of a Royal Commission which reported in 1969.

Voters

By 1914 about seven million men could vote in national elections; in 1832 this right had been given to men who paid £10 a year in rates on their houses; in 1867 the right had been extended to all men who paid rates in boroughs and in 1884 ratepayers living outside the towns (the so-called 'county voter'). In 1918 the government gave the vote to all women over the age of thirty and so about eight million women were allowed to vote—a reward for their work during the war

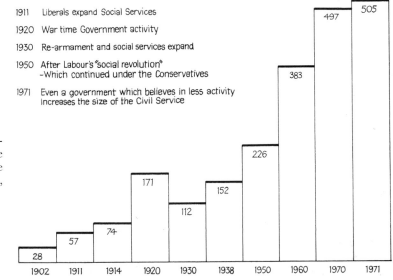

Numbers employed in non-industrial Civil Service (excluding Post Office and the Nationalised industries) in 1,000's

1911   Liberals expand Social Services

1920   War time Government activity

1930   Re-armament and social services expand

1950   After Labour's "social revolution"
       –Which continued under the Conservatives

1971   Even a government which believes in less activity
       increases the size of the Civil Service

1 As the government takes on an increasingly active role in the country's life, there have to be more civil servants to staff the various departments—of housing, health, pensions and so on.

Year	1902	1911	1914	1920	1930	1938	1950	1960	1970	1971
	28	57	74	171	112	152	226	383	497	505

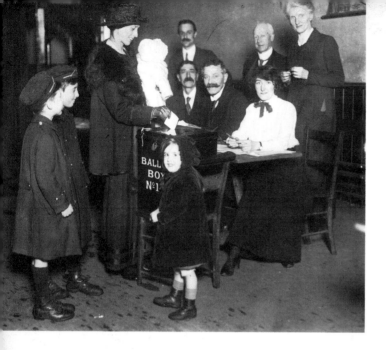

2 In 1918 women over 30 were given the right to vote at Parliamentary elections; in 1928 the same right was extended to women when they reached the age of twenty-one—only then were they given the same political rights as men.

(Chapter 3, Picture 1). It is too often forgotten that this Reform Act (1918) also gave the vote to about six million men over the age of twenty-one. In 1928 all women over the age of twenty-one were allowed to vote (Picture 2). By 1972 the right to vote has been extended to people aged eighteen.

Increased government activity

By 1914 the government had begun to take an active part in the life of the British people; at first the activity had been concerned with the environment in which people lived and worked; then it had spread and the government was involved in the building of libraries, and schools, housing and boating pools (Book 2, Chapter 6). Finally, after 1906 the government began to be concerned with providing a personal and often cash service to the less well-off: the old, the sick and the unemployed.

3 The Dounreay atomic energy reactor which is part of the property owned by the Atomic Energy Authority under the control of the Ministry of Technology.

4 A war-time ration book. When goods were scarce the government adopted a system of rationing so that everyone would get a share of what was available.

During the First World War (1914–18) the government became increasingly involved in the nation's life. Food and other goods were rationed (Picture 4); the coal and the railway industries were brought under government control while men were conscripted into the armed forces when the volunteer system failed to provide enough men (Picture 8). This increased activity was forced on the unwilling Liberal government by the need to win the War; Prime Minister Asquith proved unwilling to take all the steps necessary to mobilise the nation's resources—in keeping with his ideas of what Liberalism meant. Other Liberals had different ideas. Under the leadership of Lloyd George these New Liberals believed that freedom for the poor, the unemployed, the old and the sick required an increase in State activity, in taxation, and in the numbers of Civil Servants; they also realised that it would involve a loss of freedom for other people—who would not be as free to do what they liked with their money (some of which would be taken away in taxation) or with their industry, some of which come under government control.

This clash between the Old and the New Liberals had started before 1914, continued during the war and split the Liberal Party in 1916. The Party never recovered from this split and it was replaced by the new Labour Party which, in 1924, formed its first government under Ramsey MacDonald.

Conservative-dominated governments ruled Britain in much of the inter-war period (1918–39) and throughout this period there was a steady growth in the part played by government in the nation's life. There were a succession of Housing Acts (Chapter 5, Picture 2), an extension of the Unemployment Insurance system to cover nearly every working man (Chapter 2, Picture 6); the

47

5 The Abbey steelworks, Port Talbot, was one of the new works built in the immediate post-war years by a government anxious to make Britain great again. The use of scarce materials in such projects meant that there was less available for other, less important, projects—such as the production of cars and household goods. When the new steelworks began to produce in the early 1950s more of these goods became available—and the British people 'never had it so good'.

pension system was widened to include widows, and among the new Ministries created in this period was the Ministry of Transport—responsible for road building and the attempt to cope with the growth of the motor car (Chapter 4, Picture 3). In an attempt to help the people in the depressed areas, the government tried to persuade some of the developing industries to build factories in such areas (Chapter 2, Picture 7), and it nationalised the broadcasting system—so creating the BBC. It also brought into being State-owned airlines to help develop this new form of transport.

During the Second World War (1939–45) there was a further increase in the

6 An example of the modern public library. The library service is one provided by the local government, paid for out of taxes and rates and enjoyed by millions—unlike the private enterprise library of the early nineteenth century (Book 1, Chapter 1, Picture 9).

role of the government. Once again industry was controlled, food and other goods rationed, men and women conscripted for the Forces and for essential work. This control of the nation's resources by an increasing number of government Ministers and civil servants was accepted as being necessary to defeat Hitler. By 1945 many people were beginning to ask whether a similar use of the nation's resources might not be necessary in order to defeat other enemies. Sir William Beveridge (Chapter 5, Picture 4), produced his Report on Social Insurance in which he wrote about five Giant Evils: Disease, Idleness, Squalor, Want and Ignorance. He showed how government action could defeat each of these Evils and so make life better for a larger number of people.

The spread of ideas such as these was a major reason for the Labour Party's victory in the Election of 1945 (Chapter 1, Picture 6). Many people believed that the Labour Party would take whatever action was required to make life better. In fact, since 1945 both Labour and Conservative governments have followed roughly the same sorts of policies. Both have tried to make sure that there is a high level of employment. One way of doing this has been for the government to take over certain industries such as coal (Chapter 2, Picture 2) and the railways and to spend a good deal of money on their modernisation. This has provided work for many people in the engineering, building and machine tool industries. Another way is for the government to provide the money for the development of new industries (Picture 3), or for new developments in existing industries (Picture 5, and Chapter 4, Pictures 6 and 8), so creating work for millions of people in the electrical, aircraft and engineering industries. Increased government spending

7 Refuse disposal in the 1950s, one of the essential but still poorly paid services provided by the local authority.

8 Volunteers queuing to enlist at a recruiting office in Hammersmith in 1915.

on housing (Chapter 5, Pictures 7 and 9), and on the nation's health (Chapter 5, Picture 6) has been equalled by increased government help to Britain's farmers (Chapter 3, Pictures 5 and 7), who have bought an increasing amount of machinery and created employment for many people.

All this increased expenditure has led to an increase in the level of taxation, part of which goes to pay for the larger number of civil servants (Picture 1), part of which comes back to the taxpayer in the form of cheap food, better health services, improved local government services and more schools (Chapter 10). As the country has become richer (Chapter 1, Picture 11), so successive governments of every sort have been able to spend more money on creating a better life for the people. This would have been impossible without the industrial changes which have helped to make the country richer and have also helped to make it one in which there is a fairer distribution of the nation's income than there was in 1914. Now we have an increasing number of car owners, holiday takers, buyers of household luxuries; in 1914 over one-third of the population was described as 'poor'. There are, unfortunately, many sections of the British people who are still poor in 1972. There are millions who are badly housed (Chapter 5, Picture 8) and millions of poor families (Chapter 7, Picture 10) whose incomes are very low. But at least, unlike 1914, the nation is not only aware of these less well-off people but seems more willing to do something for them than was the case in 1914. A richer nation has also become a more caring nation, willing to devote an increasing part of its national income to helping the less well-off.

The Young Historian

1. Look at Picture 1. Find out from Chapters 3, 4 and 5 the names of three Ministries in which some of these civil servants are working. Why has this growth given women a greater chance of getting a job?
2. In Picture 3 you can see one of the stations of an industry owned by the nation. Name three other nationalised industries and find out when they were nationalised.
3. During the war there was a smaller supply of goods available for the general public (Chapter 1, Picture 5). Why did the government issue ration books (Picture 4)? Find out the size of the weekly ration of (i) butter (ii) sugar (iii) meat.
4. Since 1945 every government has tried to prevent a return of mass unemployment. One way of doing this was to build new works (Picture 5). How does the building of such a works create employment for (i) a steelworks in Sheffield, (ii) a building contractor? How does this steelworks add to the national income when it is completed?
5. Look again at Chapters 3, 4 and 5. Can you say why post-war governments have spent more money than pre-war governments? In spite of this increased spending (and taxation) people still have more money to spend than they had before 1939? Why?
6. Many men thought that women should not be allowed to vote (Picture 2): many adults thought that 18-year olds should not have been given the vote. Write a short speech in favour of or against either votes for women or votes for 18-year olds.
7. In 1970 the government appointed a Minister of the Environment. How does Picture 7 show that such a Ministry was necessary? Why will his appointment probably lead to an increase in taxation?
8. Find out from people who were alive at the time either (i) what it was like in the 1930s or (ii) what they remember about the war. If you can meet enough older people, you might be able to make a scrapbook of their memories.

7 Poverty and Unemployment

By 1914 the government had begun to accept some responsibility for helping some of the nation's poor (Book 2, Chapter 7). During the war (1914–18) many people enjoyed a higher standard of living than they had ever known. There was full employment as the government persuaded industrialists to produce an increasing volume of war material; many women went to work alongside their husbands and sons (Chapter 3, Picture 1), and the families of men in the armed forces received a weekly allowance from the government so that their income was often higher than it had been in peacetime.

But in 1921 this new-found prosperity came to a sudden end. British exporters found it increasingly difficult to sell their goods overseas (Chapters 1 and 2), so that there was a good deal of unemployment in the industries concerned with exporting (Chapter 1, Picture 2). Thousands of ex-servicemen who had been promised a 'country fit for heroes to live in' were thrown out of work and joined the millions of former munition workers, coal miners, shipbuilders, and others, in the dole queues (Picture 1). In 1911 Lloyd George had started the National Insurance scheme to help the unemployed in three trades (Book 2, Chapter 7): in 1918 this scheme was extended to cover the workers in the munition industries and ex-servicemen. When these men were unemployed they could receive insurance benefit for fifteen weeks only; after this, if they were still out of work, they were supposed to approach the Boards of Guardians. These Poor Law authorities were

1 The dole queue was a feature of life in the 1920s and 1930s when millions of men were unemployed and few married women went to work.

2 Lowly-paid workers can afford only a poor quality home—and this affects the health of the family as well as the educational opportunities of the children.

incapable of dealing with the huge numbers of unemployed in the depressed areas (Picture 9); in some places over half the working population was out of work—and no Board of Guardians could be expected to cope with this. The government realised this and changed the National Insurance system so that men were allowed to continue to draw unemployment relief from the Labour Exchange after their fifteen weeks had run out. This was the 'dole' or hand-out which kept millions of families from starvation in the inter-war period.

For the unemployed, life was very hard; many could afford little, if any, rent (Picture 2) and lived in squalid conditions. Unlike the prosperous workers in the new industries (Chapters 1 and 2) they had little to spend on food, (Picture 4), or clothing, furniture or leisure. The government tried to persuade the owners of the new industries—such as chemicals, cars and light engineering—to build factories in the depressed areas. But the government's efforts were very limited; they did not feel it right to force an industrialist to move nor did they take powers to stop an industrialist building a factory in an area where there was little unemployment.

For the unemployed there was charity (Pictures 3 and 4) provided by churches and chapels, philanthropic societies and agencies such as the Salvation Army. But there was no work and seemingly no chance of work for the two million or so out of work in the mid 1930s. Then came the threat of war; the government saw the need to spend more money on rearmament and there was work for coal miners,

3 The Salvation Army was one of the bodies which tried to provide food and shelter for the poor, the homeless and the vagrant.

4 A soup queue, 1921. Another example of the attempt by charity to help the millions of poor people.

steelworkers, shipbuilders and others (Picture 5). When war finally came (1939) it helped create even more employment—for people in the forces, women in the factories and farms, and workers in industry working to defeat Hitler.

In 1942 Sir William Beveridge presented his Report on the Social Insurance schemes (Chapter 5, Picture 4) and showed how the evils of Want and Idleness could be dealt with. The wartime government accepted some of his ideas immediately; the family allowances system was introduced before the end of the war (Picture 6) and was a great help to the mothers of large families. Since 1945 both Labour and Conservative governments have tried to prevent unemployment: they have taken over some industries and spent vast sums of money on their modernisation (Chapter 2, Picture 2 and Chapter 6, Picture 3); they have helped private industry to develop some projects such as Concorde (Chapter 2, Picture 4) and have given tax relief to private industry to encourange investment. Every new machine, house, school, steelworks or oil refinery has meant work for millions of people in a wide variety of industries.

Until 1970 the country had never had more than about two per cent of its working population out of work—never more than about 600,000 people. On the other hand, millions of families now have more than one wage earner since mothers (Chapter 9, Picture 10) go to work in many industries and occupations. Full employment has led to high wages and high wages have led to millions of

5 Work at last—in wartime.

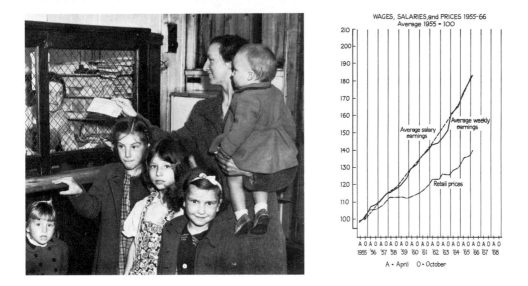

WAGES, SALARIES, and PRICES 1955-66
Average 1955 = 100

Average salary earnings

Average weekly earnings

Retail prices

A O A O A O A O A O A O A O A O A O A O A O A O A O A O
1955 '56 '57 '58 '59 '60 '61 '62 '63 '64 '65 '66 '67 '68

A - April   O - October

6 *(left)* The introduction of a system of Family Allowances was one of the social reforms made by the Churchill government in 1945 just before the General Election which returned a Labour government under which the first allowances were paid.

7 *(right)* Since 1945 the country has experienced a constant rise in prices (or inflation). Many workers, however, have managed to maintain an even higher rise in their wages—and so managed to raise their living standards.

people being able to afford a very high standard of living, (Chapter 9, Picture 3). Some unemployment is inevitable in an industrialised society; some industries must decline as others expand, some men must be thrown out of work as new methods of production are introduced. But since 1945 the government has paid a high level of unemployment benefit and since 1966 men have received unemployment benefit related to the amount they were earning, instead of receiving a flat rate benefit. In addition, the government has opened thirty or more Retraining Centres (Picture 8) where people can be retrained to do alternative jobs.

In 1972 no one lives at the level described by Rowntree when writing of the poor in York in 1902 (Book 2, Chapter 7). Today the poor are fewer than they were in 1900 when they made up about one-third of the working population. Today also the poor are better off than they were in 1900. But the rest of the working population is better off than it was in 1900 and the poor appear to be even poorer today compared with their wealthier mates than they did in 1900 when the majority were poor. This greater relative poverty makes poverty an even greater hardship today than it was in 1900. The thousands of men getting low wages in unskilled jobs (Picture 10), the millions of old people who find it difficult to live on their old age pensions, the many large families trying to get by on one income, these are the new poor for whom Britain has not yet learned to do enough. For such people the affluent society is almost meaningless; in their homes (Chapter 5, Picture 8), they do not have the symbols of affluence—the washing machines and refrigerators, the fitted carpets and the television sets.

8 *(left)* A government retraining centre where some unemployed men can receive a training to fit them for a new job.

9 The extent of unemployment in the 1930s can be judged from this illustration.

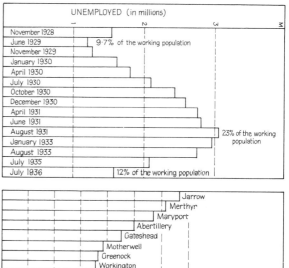

UNEMPLOYED (in millions)			
	1	2	3 M
November 1928			
June 1929	9·7% of the working population		
November 1929			
January 1930			
April 1930			
July 1930			
October 1930			
December 1930			
April 1931			
June 1931			
August 1931		23% of the working population	
January 1933			
August 1933			
July 1935			
July 1936	12% of the working population		

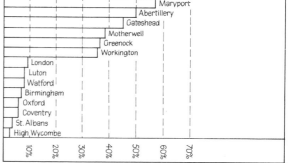

Jarrow
Merthyr
Maryport
Abertillery
Gateshead
Motherwell
Greenock
Workington
London
Luton
Watford
Birmingham
Oxford
Coventry
St. Albans
High Wycombe

10% 20% 30% 40% 50% 60% 70%

10 In the middle of the affluent society of the 1950s and 1960s there were still very many poor families with a very low standard of living.

As the country has become richer it has become possible for many of the ordinary people to help themselves to higher wages and a greater share in the national income and they enjoy a high standard of living. It has also been possible for the government to spend increasing sums in helping the less well-off—the old, the sick, the unemployed. But in 1972 there is strong evidence that not enough is being done. One hope for the future is that a richer society has become a caring society; we can hope that it will learn to care sufficiently for those who are less able to help themselves.

The Young Historian

1. Find out how much was paid in Family Allowances in 1945 (Picture 6) for a family of three children. The average manual worker's wage in 1945 was £4. By what percentage did the family income increase when Family Allowances were first paid?

2. Write a letter that might have been written by one of the returned and unemployed soldiers (Picture 1). (See also Chapter 1, Picture 1.) Which of Beveridge's 'giant evils' would such a man have known.

3. Which sort of people had to depend on charity in the 1920s and 1930s? (Pictures 3 and 4). Why is there less of this charity in post-war Britain?

4. You can see from Picture 7 that both prices and wages have risen since 1945. Which one has grown most rapidly? What does this tell you about the people's standards of living? Name three things on which the wealthier British are spending their money.

5. Some people say that 'there are no poor now—or maybe a few only'. Do you agree? Can you name three groups of people who still have a low standard of living?

6. When was unemployment at its highest peak (Picture 9)? Why was some of this caused by the low prices being paid for British imports (Chapter 3, Picture 3)? Who gained from these falling prices?

7. Paint or draw (i) the home of the unemployed in the 1930s (Picture 2) and (ii) his home after he found another job.

8. Why are there fewer coal miners today than there were in 1914? Can you suggest how the development of (i) nylon and (ii) polythene may lead to unemployment for some people? Why are retraining centres (Picture 8) very necessary in a modern society?

8 Trade Unions and Working Conditions

Changing industrial conditions

During the last sixty years there has been a steady and continual decrease in the number of people doing physically hard and dirty jobs. There are 600,000 fewer coalworkers now than in 1914 (Chapter 2, Picture 1); only about half as many shipbuilding workers as in 1914 and much less than half the number of farm labourers. On the other hand there has been a steady increase in the number of skilled and semi-skilled workers on assembly lines (Chapter 2, Picture 3). An increasing part of industry has become steadily more automated (Picture 8) so that machines are doing the work previously done by workmen. One result of this development has been the need to provide a more educated workforce—to design, build, maintain and operate such machines.

Service industries

As Britain has become steadily richer, her more affluent people have been able to afford to spend money on non-productive industries which provide a service rather than an article. There has been a rise in the number of people working to provide these services, such as hairdressing (Chapter 2, Picture 8), and to staff the many insurance companies required to cater for the insuring of our lives, houses and cars (Chapter 4, Picture 3). By 1914 the large departmental stores such as Selfridge's and Bentall's (Book 2, Chapter 1, Picture 7) were a feature of Britain's large towns and cities. Since 1914 there has been a huge rise in the number of such shops; in the 1920s and 1930s the American firm, Woolworth's, opened a store in most towns; since 1945 the affluent customers have created the demand for shops to provide them with their clothes, kitchenware, household goods and furniture (Chapter 9, Picture 3). The catering firm of Lyons was among the first to provide a café/restaurant service for the middle classes (Pictures 5 and 6); since the mid-1950s the number of cafés and restaurants has increased as more people have learned to enjoy a wider variety of foreign foods.

Office workers

By 1914 there were a number of firms which had large office staffs working in very comfortable conditions (Book 2, Chapter 2, Picture 8). Since 1914 there has been a steady increase in the number of such firms and such offices; in London there are the giant office blocks of Shell House and ICI; in Newcastle there is the giant block for the people working in the Health Service; both government and private

LUNCH EDITION.

Emergency   Bulletin.

No. 3.   THURSDAY MAY 6th.   Price **One Penny**

Latest Strike News

In the House of Commons **yesterday the** Home Secretary said railway conditions **have improved. Food** supply is satisfactory **and** appealed to the country to enrol as special constables.

The general position throughout the Country is reported to be very satisfactory. **There has been** a large increase in the number of trains run and it is hoped to improve on the Tube service in **London to-day.**

The Daily Mail says that the Trade Union Congress, realizing that the Strike is likely **to fail have been** making desperate efforts **to find ground to call it off.**

Mr. Salatvala the Communist **M.P.** who was arrested on Monday and remanded on bail **will appear at** Bow Street Police Court today

The arrangements made by the Goverment for food Supply Services are running smoothly **and no** shortage is anticipated.

TRAFFIC ANNOUNCEMENTS.

Over 300 **trains were run on the** L.M. & S. Ryl. yesterday and the number will be greatly increased **to-day.** Electric trains will run between Euston and Watford at 14 minutes intervals from 7.45, a.m. onwards. Some of **the principal** long distance trains will also run. Met Rly. Trains will run between Baker Street and Harrow to-day **every 15 minutes untill** 10.30. p.m. and every 10 minues between Edgware Road and Aldgate.   Tube Railways, It is hoped to run **a normal service** on the Central London Ryl tomorrow or Friday at latest, a four minute service will run between Wood **Lane and the City** and several additional Stations opened.

MOTOR BUSES.   Over 800 Buses will be running in London

YESTERDAY'S RACING AT CHESTER,

2.0 Jenny Deans 1, 1-7 2 ran.   2.30 Little Grey 10-11 7 ran

3.15 Chester Cup. Hiddenis 1 11-2   Vemillion Pencil 2   4 1   Izie 3rd   100 6

3.50. Naptha 2 1 4.20. Arc En Ceil 3 1 5.20. Maritza 2 5

FURTHER RACING CANCELLED.

The Stewards of the Jockey Club have cancelled all racing until further notice.

STOP PRESS NEWS.

NO SETTLEMENT IN SIGHT.

Despite informal conversations between members of the Government and Trade Union Leaders no progress was made yesterday towards a settlement.

It was announced that the government is determined that no resumption of negotation can be considered by it until the notice ordering the General Strike has been withdrawn.

Four Tram Cars travelling to the City yesterday carrying in all only two passengers were attacked and several windows were broken.

It is announced that the Goverment will not allow any victimisation of any worker who remains at his post during crisis and that no settlement will be agreed to that does not provide for this.

Work has been resumed in the Cardiff Docks. A large number of Signalmen have reported for duty unconditionly all over the Country.

Conditions in Bradford and Birmingham are practically normal, except for Tramway Services.

Printed & Published by Chandler & Co., 8, Broad Street, W.1.

CIVIL WAR PLOT BY SOCIALISTS' MASTERS.

MOSCOW ORDERS TO OUR REDS.

GREAT PLOT DISCLOSED YESTERDAY.

"PARALYSE THE ARMY AND NAVY."

AND MR. MACDONALD WOULD LEND RUSSIA OUR MONEY!

DOCUMENT ISSUED BY FOREIGN OFFICE

AFTER "DAILY MAIL" HAD SPREAD THE NEWS.

A "very secret" letter of instruction from Moscow, which we publish below, discloses a great Bolshevik plot to paralyse the British Army and Navy and to plunge the country into civil war.

The letter is addressed by the Bolsheviks of Moscow to the Soviet Government's servants in Great Britain, the Communist Party, who in turn are the masters of Mr. Ramsay MacDonald's Government, which has signed a treaty with Moscow whereby the Soviet is to be guaranteed a "loan" of millions of British money.

The letter is signed by Zinoviev, the Dictator of Petrograd, President of the Third (Moscow) International, and is addressed to McManus, the British representative on the executive of that International, who returned from Moscow to London on September 18 to take part in the general election campaign.

Our information is that official copies of the letter, which is dated September 15, were delivered to the Foreign Secretary, Mr. Ramsay MacDonald, and the Home Secretary, Mr. Arthur Henderson, immediately after it was received some weeks ago. On Wednesday afternoon copies were officially circulated by the Executive authorities to high officers of the Army and Navy.

A copy of the document came into the possession of The Daily Mail. We felt it our duty to make it public. We circulated private copies to other London morning newspapers yesterday afternoon, and on the Foreign Office decided to issue it, together with a protest yesterday, which the British Government has sent to M. Rakovski, the Bolshevik Chargé d'Affaires in London.

The salient passages of Moscow's plot letter are:

Armed warfare must be preceded by a struggle against the inclinations to compromise which are embedded among the majority of British workmen, against the ideas of evolution and peaceful extermination of capitalism.

Only then will it be possible to count on complete success of an armed insurrection.

From your last report it is evident that agitation-propaganda work in the Army is weak, and the Navy a very little better. . . . It would be desirable to have [propaganda-agitation] cells in all the units of the troops, among factories working on munitions and at military store depots.

The military section of the British Communist Party further suffers from a lack of specialists, the future directors of the British Red Army . . . . . It is time you thought of forming such a group.

The British protest is signed, in the absence of the Foreign Secretary, Mr. MacDonald, by Mr. J. D. Gregory, Permanent Assistant Secretary of the Foreign Office. It requests a reply "without delay."

The text of this protest is in another column.

THE BRITISH RED ARMY.

OUR COMMUNISTS TOLD TO FIND GENERAL STAFF.

The text of the civil war document is:

EXECUTIVE COMMITTEE   VERY SECRET.
Third
COMMUNIST INTERNATIONAL
      PRESIDIUM   TO THE CENTRAL COMMITTEE
Sept. 15th. 1924.   BRITISH COMMUNIST PARTY.
MOSCOW

Comrades,
The time is approaching for the Parliament of England to consider the treaty concluded between the Governments of Great Britain and the S.S.R. for the purpose of ratification. The fierce campaign raised by the British bourgeoisie around the question shows that the majority of the same, together with reactionary circles, are against the Treaty for the purpose of breaking off an agreement consolidating the ties between the proletariats of the two countries leading to the restoration of normal relations between England and the S.S.R.

The proletariat of Great Britain, which pronounced its weighty word when danger threatened of a break-off of the past negotiations, and compelled the Government of MacDonald to conclude the Treaty, will show the greatest possible energy in the further struggle for ratification and against the endeavours of British capitalists to compel Parliament to annul it.

It is indispensable to stir up the masses of the British proletariat, to bring into movement the army of unemployed proletarians, whose position can be improved only after a loan has been granted to the S.S.R. for the restoration of her economics and when business collaboration between the British and Russian proletariats has been put in order. It is imperative that the group in the Labour Party sympathising with the Treaty should bring increased pressure to bear upon the Government and parliamentary circles in favour of the ratification of the Treaty.

Keep close observation over the leaders of the Labour Party, because these may easily be found in the leading strings of the bourgeoisie. The foreign policy of the Labour Party as it is already represents an inflexible copy of the policy of the Curzon Government. Organise a campaign of disclosure of the foreign policy of MacDonald.

ARMED INSURRECTION.

The IKKI [Executive Committee, Third (Communist) International] will willingly place at your disposal the wide material in its possession regarding the activities of British imperialism in the Middle and Far East. In the meanwhile, however, strain every nerve in the struggle for the ratification of the Treaty, in favour of a continuation of negotiations regarding the regulation of relations between the S.S.S.R. and England. A settlement of relations between the two countries will assist in the revolutionising of the international and British proletariat not less than a successful rising in any of the working districts of England, as the establishment of close contact between the British and Russian proletariat, the exchange of delegations and workers, etc., will make it possible for us to extend and develop the propaganda of ideas of Leninism in England and the Colonies. Armed warfare must be preceded by a struggle against the inclinations to compromise which are embedded among the majority of British workmen, against the ideas of evolution and peaceful extermination of capitalism. Only then will it be possible to count upon complete success of an armed insurrection.

In Ireland and the Colonies the case is different; there is a national question, and this represents too great a factor for success for us to waste time on a prolonged preparation of the working class.

But even in England, as in other countries where the workers are politically developed, events themselves may more rapidly revolutionise the working masses than propaganda. For instance, a strike movement, repressions by the Government, etc.

From your last report it is evident that agitation - propaganda work in the Army is weak, in the Navy a very little better. Your explanation that the quality of the members attracted justifies the quantity is right in principle, nevertheless it would be desirable to have cells in all the units of the troops, particularly among those quartered in the large centres of the country, and also among factories working on munitions and at military store depots. We request that the most particular attention be paid to these latter.

A CLASS WAR.

In the event of danger of war, with the aid of the latter and in contact with the transport workers, it is possible to paralyse all the military preparations of the bourgeoisie, and make a start in turning an imperialist war into a class war. Now more than ever we should be on our guard. Attempts at intervention in China show that world imperialism is still full of vigour and is once more making endeavours to restore its shaken position and cause a new war, which as the final objective is to bring about the break-up of the Russian proletariat and the suppression of the budding world revolution, and further would lead to the enslavement of the colonial peoples. "Danger of War," "The Bourgeoisie seek War: Capital fresh Markets"—these are the slogans which you must familiarise the masses with, with which you must go to work into the mass of the proletariat. These slogans will open to you the doors of comprehension of the masses, will help you to capture them and march under the banner of Communism.

The Military Section of the British Communist Party, so far as we are aware, further suffers from a lack of specialists, the future directors of the British Red Army.

It is time you thought of forming such a group, which, together with the leaders, might be, in the event of an outbreak of active strife, the brain of the military organisation of the party.

Go attentively through the lists of the military "cells" detailing from them the more energetic and capable men, turn attention to the more talented military specialists, who have for one reason or another left the Service and hold Socialist views. Attract them into the ranks of the Communist Party if they desire honestly to serve the proletariat and desire in the future to direct not the blind mechanical forces in the service of the bourgeoisie but a national army.

Form a directing operative head of the Military Section.

Do not put this off to a future moment, which may be pregnant with events and catch you unprepared.

Desiring you all success, both in organisation and in your struggle,

With Communist Greetings,
President of the Presidium of the IKKI,
ZINOVIEV,
Member of the Presidium,
McManus,
Secretary, KUUSINEN.

FOREIGN OFFICE PROTEST.

REPLY WITHOUT DELAY REQUESTED.

The following is the text of the letter sent yesterday by Mr. J. D. Gregory to M. Rakovski, the Chargé d'Affaires in London of the Soviet Union:—

FOREIGN OFFICE,
October 24, 1924.

Sir,—I have the honour to invite your attention to the enclosed copy of a letter which has been received by the Central Committee of the British Communist Party from the Presidium of the Executive Committee of the Communist International, over the signature of Monsieur Zinoviev, its president, dated September 15.

The letter contains instructions to British subjects to work for the violent overthrow of existing institutions in this country, and for the subversion of His Majesty's armed forces as a means to that end.

2. It is my duty to inform you that his Majesty's Government cannot allow this propaganda and must regard it as a direct interference from outside in British domestic affairs.

3. No one who understands the constitution and the relationships of the Communist International will doubt its intimate connection and contact with the Soviet Government. No Government will ever tolerate an arrangement with a foreign Government by which the latter is in formal diplomatic relations with a correct kind with it, while at the same time a propagandist body practically connected with that foreign Government encourages and even orders subjects of the former to plot and plan revolutions for its overthrow.

Such conduct is not only a grave departure from the rules of international comity, but a violation of specific and solemn undertakings repeatedly given to his Majesty's Government.

4. So recently as June 4 of last year the Soviet Government made the following solemn agreement with his Majesty's Government:—

The Soviet Government undertakes not to support with funds or in any other form persons or bodies or agencies

or institutions whose aim is to spread discontent or to foment rebellion in any part of the British Empire . . . and to impress upon its officers and officials the full and continuous observance of these conditions.

8. Moreover, in the Treaty which his Majesty's Government recently concluded with your Government, full further provision was made for the faithful execution of an analogous undertaking which is essential to the existence of good and friendly relations between the two countries.

His Majesty's Government mean that these undertakings shall be carried out both in the letter and in the spirit, and cannot accept the contention that while the Soviet Government undertakes obligations, a political body, as powerful as itself, is to be allowed to conduct a propaganda and support it with money.

6. I should be obliged if you would be good enough to let me have the observations of your Government on this subject without delay.

I have the honour to be, with high consideration, Sir,
Your Obedient Servant,
(In the absence of the Secretary of State)
M. C. Rakovski,   (Sd.) J. D. GREGORY,
Etc., etc., etc.

THE MASTER ASSASSIN.

ZINOVIEV WHO SIGNED DEATH WARRANTS OF THOUSANDS.

Under the Czars, Zinoviev, who is 41, was associated with the Terrorist group who were responsible for all political assassinations in Russia. In 1908 he was arrested for being concerned in publishing a paper which incited the readers to a bloody revolution and the entire destruction of the bourgeoisie.

Between 1915 and 1917 he denounced the Allies on every possible occasion, and by means of smuggled correspondence got into touch with British pacifists. Getting back to Russia in March 1917 he helped to demoralise the Russian army, and on the success of the Bolshevist coup d'état became the leader of the Petrograd Soviet and the master assassin.

As the head of the Petrograd Commune he signed the death warrants of thousands of men, women, and people. He organised the Secret Police of Petrograd.

AGITATIONS OF McMANUS.

Arthur McManus started life as a fitter at Liverpool. For his activities on the Clyde during the war, as editor of the Glasgow Socialist, he was deported to Edinburgh.

At one time he was in touch with the Industrial Workers of the World, an organisation concerned in "general outrages in the United States and Australia.

After a visit to Russia last year he said there was a sense of security there that existed in no other country.

He is chairman of the British Communist Party.

LATEST NEWS

SPEAKER'S DEATH AT MEETING.

When concluding a speech in support of Mr. Frank Hannon, Conservative candidate in the Ladywood division of Birmingham, at St. Stephen's School, Camden-street, Mr. T. McGhee, last night, ex-Councillor Thomas McHoy, of Blakey, collapsed and died.

He had just pronounced the words "for God, for King, and for country" when he fell back in his chair. Four members of the audience fainted.

THE PREMIER'S TRUST.

Hours after the Foreign Office yesterday had sent the note to the Bolsheviks stating that their "Very Secret" instruction is "a violation of specific and solemn undertakings repeatedly given to his Majesty's Government," Mr. Ramsay MacDonald, Secretary of State for Foreign Affairs, said at Talbach, in his Aberavon constituency:

I have no doubt that Russia will carry out the Treaties we have with her.

£5,000 OR £5 A WEEK FOR LIFE.

"DAILY MAIL" ELECTION COMPETITION.

POST FORMS NOW.

To-day the entry-form for the Daily Mail's great Election Competition is at the top of Column 4, Page 2.

To-morrow it will be printed in every copy of The Weekly Dispatch, and it will also appear in The Daily Mail on Monday and Tuesday next. These will represent the final chances of winning the great prize of

FIVE THOUSAND POUNDS OR £5 A WEEK FOR LIFE.

Forms which have already been completed should be sent at once to the address given below.

There is no entry fee, and the prize must be won.

Cut out the form carefully, setting against the name of each party the number of candidates you estimate will be elected holding those political views. Forecasts must be sent to—

"ELECTION COMPETITION,
THE DAILY MAIL,
7, Pilgrim-street,
LONDON, E.C. 4."

Each forecast must be on a separate entry form, cut from The Daily Mail or from The Weekly Dispatch. Forms which arrive after the first post on October 29 will be disqualified.

In the event of a tie or ties the sum of £5,000 will be divided among the successful competitors.

There are 615 seats in the House of Commons, so your estimate should add up to this total.

In the last Parliament there were, at the dissolution:—

CONSERVATIVES 257
LABOUR AND COMMUNISTS ... 192
LIBERALS 158
INDEPENDENT 7

One Conservative seat was unfilled pending a by-election.

THE ENTRY FORM AND RULES ARE AT THE TOP OF COLUMN 4, PAGE 2.

21 DEATHS MYSTERY.

14 WOMEN VICTIMS IN A MOTOR-SHIP WRECK.

FROM OUR OWN CORRESPONDENT
RIGA, Friday.

Riga is mystified by the wreck of a motor-assisted sailing vessel, the Belinder, which ran ashore in Riga bay in yesterday's storm. Twenty-one persons lost their lives, including 14 women.

Twelve bodies have been washed ashore, and 9 people were found dead in the hold of the vessel apparently suffocated by petrol fumes.

Among the dead are the crew of three. The authorities are investigating the matter and believe that the drinking of vodka, the alcoholic drink commonly consumed in Russia, is the cause.

Continued from Preceding Column,
which is in direct violation of the official agreement.

The Soviet Government either has or has not the power to make such agreements. If it has the power it is its duty to carry them out and see that the other parties are not deceived. If it has not this power and if responsibilities which belong to the State in other countries are in Russia in the keeping of private and irresponsible bodies the Soviet Government ought not to make agreements which it knows it cannot carry out.

HANGED IN PAIRS.

FOUR BANK BANDITS.

FROM OUR OWN CORRESPONDENT
MONTREAL, Friday.

On two scaffolds dimly lighted by small lanterns four bandits were executed just before dawn this morning for the murder of a bank chauffeur in the "hold-up" of a Bank of Hochlaga collection car in April.

The men were Louis Morel, a former Montreal detective; Tony Frank, known as the King of the Underworld; Frank Gambino, and Giuseppe Serafini, who had just returned from his honeymoon in Italy.

Morel, once a famous athlete, shout like a Greek statue on the scaffold, Gambino fainted, but rallied; Frank faced death bravely; and Serafini kissed the priest and the gaol governor passionately after. The prison was heavily guarded by constables with fixed bayonets, and motor-cycle detachments patrolled all the roads.

DE VALERA ARRESTED.

ULSTER POLICE ACTION.

Mr. de Valera, the Irish Republican leader, was arrested by the Ulster authorities last night when he entered the town hall at Newry, County Down, to address a meeting in support of the Republicans.

He was first served with an expulsion order by armed police. He refused to obey it and was bundled unceremoniously out of the hall. Miss Mary MacSwiney, one of his followers, tried to greet him, but the police intervened. Revolvers were drawn when the crowd showed signs of surging towards the constables.

De Valera's disguise consisted of leaving off his large, horn-rimmed spectacles. The Ulster police knew him only by his newspaper portraits, in which the spectacles figure prominently.

Newry had been agog with excitement at the prospect of Mr. de Valera attempting to elude the authorities and address the meeting.

The chief Republican secret agent (at Dublin) has sent a telegram to the British Prime Minister and the Home Secretary relating to the arrest of de Valera and declaring: "This outrage was impossible without the connivance of the British Government, which decreed the elections, and which is responsible for proper conduct of them."

YOUR VOTE.

HOW AND WHERE TO RECORD IT.

It is the patriotic duty of every qualified man and woman to vote next Wednesday.

If you have any doubt about YOUR eligibility you should go to-day to the nearest principal post office and ask to see the local register of parliamentary electors. If your name is in this list you are entitled to vote. Your name will appear on the register of the district in which you resided on June 15 last.

WHERE TO VOTE.

Full information about the time and the place, the polling-booth, to vote, will be given to you at the nearest Conservative or Liberal committee room.

The ballot is absolutely secret. A ballot paper is handed to the voter at the polling booth. On this paper you must write a cross (X) in the space provided on the right-hand side of the name of the candidate for whom you wish to vote. Nothing else must be written on the paper. It is important to note that the names of candidates are always arranged in alphabetical order.

PEKING CHANGES HANDS.

COUP WHILE CITY SLEPT.

GATES OPENED BY PLOTTERS.

"CHRISTIAN GENERAL'S IRONSIDES."

FROM OUR OWN CORRESPONDENT.
PEKING, Friday.

Yesterday's occupation of the capital by Feng Yu-hsiang, the "Christian general," who deserted and returned suddenly from the front with his "Ironsides," followed the entire collapse of the Peking Government forces in their fight against Chang Tso-lin, the War Lord of Manchuria.

Wu Pei-fu, the Commander-in-Chief of the Government forces, is reported to have fled aboard an Italian gunboat at Chinwangtao. Everything was arranged according to the plans of Chang Tso-lin.

The city is quiet and no trouble is anticipated.

FROM OUR OWN CORRESPONDENT.
MUKDEN, Friday.

Chang's Manchurian forces have now cut off 25,000 retreating Central Government troops between Shanhaikwan (near the Great Wall, about 200 miles east of Peking) and Chinwangtao. President Tsao Kun is a refugee in the Dutch Legation at Peking. General Wu must now surrender or fly to Japan.

FROM OUR OWN CORRESPONDENT.
MUKDEN, Friday.

The naval authorities here learn that Feng has issued a proclamation saying he intends to put an end to the war. It may also be his intention to replace the President, Tsao Kun, by Tuan Chi-jui, the former Premier.

The presidential palace is surrounded by troops. The only means of communication with Peking is by wireless.

THE PLOT.

PEKING, Friday.

A group of generals having decided to bring hostilities to an end, secretly arranged for Feng's return to take control of the city, while others took measures to prevent Wu Pei-fu re-entering it, while the city still slept, the Peking garrison troops opened the gates to Feng's men.

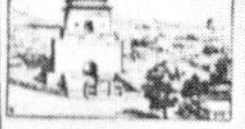

While most of the members of the Cabinet were not concerned in the plot, a group of generals of young Chinese, including Huang Fu, Minister of Education, and Dr. C. T. Wang, former Foreign Minister, took part inside Peking. This group meets in secret to arrange bringing hostilities to an end, after which it intends to call a round table conference.

The occupants of the two army stores troops having reached Peking, General Feng has a fatal command of more than 40,000 men. Not a single shot was fired either during or after the coup d'état.

President Tsao Kun has issued a mandate ordering an immediate cessation of hostilities. Wu Pei-fu is dismissed from his present post and appointed "Chief Commissioner for the development of Koko-Nor (a large salt-water lake just beyond the boundary of Kansu province). Both armies of the Peking forces and those of Chang Tso-lin are ordered to maintain the status quo.—Reuter.

3 *(left)* Ernest Bevin, General Secretary of the Transport and General Workers Union, had been one of the leaders of the General Strike. In 1940 Winston Churchill invited Bevin to join the Coalition government as Minister of Labour. In this office he was one of the main architects of Britain's victory over Hitler.

4 *(right)* Post-war governments have tried, in various ways, to halt the rise in prices and wages. The Wilson government (1964–70) set up a Prices and Incomes Board. The illustration shows the Minister in charge, George Brown, with leaders of industry and the TUC.

industry employ an ever-increasing number of office workers (Chapter 9, Picture 1).

However, there are still very many people who do a dirty and dangerous job, and very often these are the lowest-paid workers (Picture 7). In one way their difficulties are greater now than was the case in 1914 when a larger number of people did a dirty and lowly-paid job. This smaller number stands out in our present society.

Large trade unions

By 1914 there were several large trade unions such as the transport workers, railway workers and miners. But most unions then were small—the engineers had a membership of about 200,000. Most of the larger unions consisted of unskilled workers earning little money so that they could afford only a small amount in union subscriptions. Ben Tillett, the founder of the Dockers' Union (Book 2, Chapter 8, Picture 6), said that they had only 7/6 (37½p) in the kitty in 1890. These trade unions had already shown themselves to be very militant in their desire to raise people's living standards.

First World War

During the First World War (1914–18) most trade unions gave up their militancy

2 *(opposite)* The Zinoviev letter 1924 which alleged that the Labour government was a willing agent for the Russian Communist Party. The letter was probably a forgery, but the mass of middle class people wanted to believe that it was true—they suspected the Labour Party with its call for social justice.

5 'A Nippy' in one of the Lyons Cafés which were a feature of middle class life in the 1930s.

and relaxed their rules to allow women workers to do the jobs previously done by skilled or semi-skilled workmen; they did not strike for higher wages because they realised that their work was essential if the war was to be won. Their leaders hoped that from this co-operation in wartime would follow a similar co-operation with management and government after the war, which would result in better living standards. In the immediate post-war years several of the larger unions won large pay increases for their members, and Ernest Bevin (Picture 3) first came to prominence by getting a large pay increase for the dockers in 1920. However, the depression of the 1920s (Chapters 1 and 2) saw the beginning of large-scale unemployment (as exporters found it impossible to sell their goods). Both the government and the owners thought that the quickest way of bringing down the prices of British goods (and so increasing the chance of selling them abroad) was to reduce wages. This was what the coalmine owners tried to do in 1926; the trade union movement supported the miners' decision to oppose such cuts and the General Strike took place (Picture 1). The government saw this strike as a Communist attempt to overthrow the constitution (Picture 2); supported by the majority of Church leaders, lawyers and middle-class people, the government refused to discuss terms with the leaders of the Trade Union movement. These leaders, on the other hand, thought that the strike was about wage cuts; when they were persuaded that it could be seen as an attack on the constitution some of them became frightened; others realised that the government had been elected by the majority of the people while the trade union movement represented only a section of the population—they saw that the government had to govern; still other leaders were afraid that a long General Strike would run away with the unions' finances as they paid out weekly sums to the strikers.

For a variety of reasons the Trade Union leaders called off the General Strike after only ten days. The government passed the Trades Disputes Act (1927) to make sure that there would never be another General Strike. Under the leadership of people such as Bevin the union movement decided that such political strikes would not gain any benefit for the unions. They turned the union movement back again to negotiating with employers, with starting new unions for workers in the new industries (Chapter 2, Picture 3) and with trying to prove that trade unionism was not a Communist plot.

6 A menu which illustrates the price levels of the 1930s. Some people benefitted from this fall in prices and enjoyed a high standard of living.

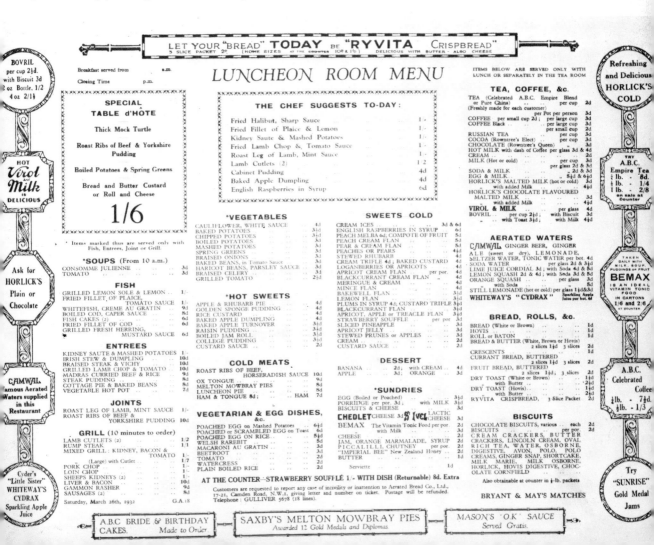

7 Some workers still have to do dirty and dangerous jobs—and for low wages. In 1970 the refuse collectors in many towns went on strike in support of a claim for a pay increase.

Second World War

During the Second World War the unions once again co-operated with the government; Bevin and other leaders were brought into the Churchill government; many of them helped Beveridge to write his Report (Chapter 5, Picture 4); he himself said that the unions were its godfathers. When the Labour government came to power in 1945 the unions agreed to co-operate to make sure that full employment for their members would not lead to inflation. However, as the national income rose (Chapter 1, Picture 11) so they demanded an increasing share for their members. As wages rose so did prices (Chapter 7, Picture 7) and while millions of workers were better off in this situation, millions of less well organised people (usually white-collared or professional workers) felt that they were losing ground as their wages and salaries were not rising as quickly as those of the members of strong unions. This is one reason why, on the one hand, trade unions had come in for a lot of criticism in the 1960s while, on the other hand, middle-class workers (including doctors, nurses, teachers and bank clerks) had begun to use the militant methods of the older unions in their attempts to get higher wages and salaries.

8 Men working in one of the modern industries receive high wages for clean and less dangerous jobs; their output is very high because of the machinery they use, so employers can afford the high wages.

Wages and inflation

As people have been paid higher wages so they have bought for themselves a share in the affluent society; they own cars and houses, they buy more goods and go on more holidays. There is, however, another side to this coin; as wages rise so do prices and as prices rise so British firms find it difficult to sell their goods abroad. But Britain has to sell abroad—to pay for the increasing imports required by the affluent workers. Several governments have tried to get the trade unions to accept some form of prices and incomes policy (Picture 4). But no government has yet succeeded in halting the circle of wage increases leading to price increases leading to wage increases and so on.

As British goods become more expensive so Britain finds herself in an almost continuous balance of payments crisis; the country which once financed the building of the world's railways and industries has since the period from 1945 been forced to borrow from the rest of the world. Twice since 1945 Britain has had to devalue its currency (Chapter 1, Picture 10) in efforts to increase its export-income to help pay for its rising level of imports.

The Young Historian

1. Find out when the Zinoviev letter was written (Picture 2). Who, according to the *Daily Mail* controlled the unions and the Labour Party?

2. Why has there been an increase in the number of people working in shops, cafés, hotels and other service industries in the twentieth century (Pictures 5 and 6)? Why is this only possible in a country with (i) a very high national income and (ii) a very good transport system (Chapter 4, Picture 4).

3. Look at the menu and the prices in a café in the 1930s (Picture 6). Find out how much you would have to pay today for one of these meals. Would you prefer to change places with people living in the 1930s?

4. Why did Winston Churchill invite Ernest Bevin to join his government in 1940? (Picture 3). Find out the names of three other Labour politicians who were in the wartime Cabinet.

5. Look again at Chapter 1, Picture 7, Chapter 2, Pictures 2 and 3, 4 and 5. Why have working conditions improved since 1914? Do you think that everyone's working conditions are good today?

6. In Chapter 7, Picture 7 we saw that many people are earning more money now than in 1945. Can you say why this has led to an increase in the imports of (i) Japanese transistor radios and (ii) oil? Why does the government want to hold down wages (Picture 4)?

7. In the past, trade unions represented only the working class. Find out the names of trade unions which represent (i) schoolteachers (ii) clerks working for the local council (iii) airline pilots. Each of these unions has either called or threatened to call strikes. Why have these middle class workers imitated the working class trade unionists?

9 Women and the Family

Women and the First World War

During the First World War (1914–18) thousands of women joined the forces, worked on farms (Chapter 3, Picture 1) or worked in industry and in all three ways made their contribution to the winning of the war. It was this rather than the militancy of Mrs Pankhurst (Book 2, Chapter 9, Picture 9) that was responsible for the government's decision to allow some women the right to vote in 1918 (Chapter 6, Picture 2). Having once enjoyed the pleasure of a salary or wage packet, many women wished to continue to work after 1918. In 1919 the government passed the Sex Disqualification Removal Act which allowed women equal rights with men in entering certain professions, particularly the legal profession. This was a help to a small number of middle-class and highly qualified women. More significantly employers began to recruit an increasing number of women workers in their offices (Picture 1) and as the country became richer so more women found work in shops (Chapter 1, Picture 8) and service industries (Chapter 8, Picture 5 and Chapter 2, Picture 8).

Women and family 1919–39

However, once a woman married and had children, most employers considered that she was unsuitable for employment. During the inter-war period (1919–39) the size of the average family went down; the working class were copying the middle class who had begun to have small families in the 1880s (Book 2, Chapter 9, Picture 1). Families with only one or two children found it easier to live through

1 Women at work in the offices of the Milk Marketing Board. As the government became increasingly active there were job opportunities for many women in the constantly growing civil service. Private industry also provided similar office jobs in the head offices of the large firms.

the depression of the 1920s and 1930s than did families with six or seven children. Indeed the families of men in steady jobs found that this was a period during which their standard of living rose. Falling prices for food and clothes (Chapter 1, Picture 3 and Chapter 3, Picture 3), meant that many of these families had money left over to spend on houses (Chapter 5, Pictures 1 and 3) and furniture, household goods often bought at Woolworth's (Chapter 1, Picture 8) and sometimes on cars or holidays (Picture 9). Indeed some women were able to give up work so that the numbers of domestic servants declined (Picture 3).

Women since the Second World War
During the Second World War there was once again a demand for women to go into the services, factories and to work on the land. However, unlike their mothers in 1918, these wartime workers found that there was plenty of work for them after the war was over. Millions of women have found work in the Civil Service (Chapter 6, Picture 1) or in one of the welfare services (Chapter 5, Picture 6). There has been an increasing demand for teachers (Chapter 10) and other social

2 A cartoon showing a charwoman and her middle class employer just after the First World War.
'Charwoman. "Please, Mum, I ain't coming to work here no more."
Mistress. "Indeed. How is that?"
Charwoman. "Well, my man's earning so much now that there's plenty coming in. Last week we was obliged to put some in the savings-bank, and I'm afraid we shall have to again *this* week."''

3 Running a home became easier with the invention of devices such as these.

4 The modern family is much smaller than the Victorian family. This means that many mothers (of one or two children) have time to spare to go to work whereas their Victorian grandmother was constantly busy looking after her larger family.

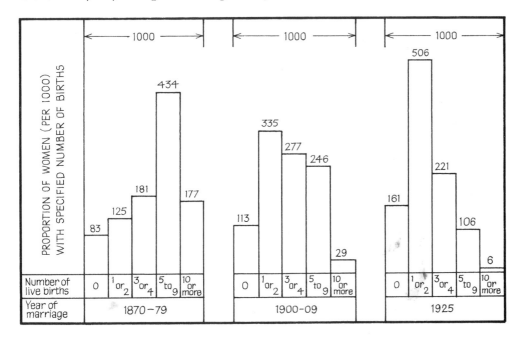

5 Smaller families, easy-to-run homes and high family incomes have allowed many women to enjoy a wide variety of leisure pursuits; some, such as the mother here, take up painting or some similar hobby.

workers as well as for women to work in offices (Picture 1), shops or one of the many service industries (Chapter 2, Picture 8). The demand for workers has been so great that employers have been anxious to take on married women—something that had only been common either in working-class Lancashire or during wartime. Now it has become a seemingly natural and inevitable part of the British way of life. About five million married women go to work each day (Picture 10).

Home and Work

It is of course much easier for the modern woman to combine her role of home-maker and worker than it would have been even in the 1930s. Her home is easier to run with its modern kitchen (Picture 3) and equipment, easily washable clothes and washing machine, easy-to-prepare foods. The modern woman has been among the greatest gainer from modern technology which has given her nylon, polythene, stainless steel, washing-up liquids, pre-prepared foods as well as a number of machines to make her work easier. In addition the modern woman, marrying earlier than her mother, has a small family who go to school by the time she is about thirty; she has a longer life span than her mother's—the modern woman can look forward to about thirty years or so of a working life is she so wishes.

Working mothers

When the mother goes to work the family benefits in many ways; her income increases the family's income and so helps to buy for the family a larger share of

6-8 *(opposite)* These are pictures taken in 1894, 1924 and 1952 of children in the same class in a London school. The social progress of the last hundred years is well illustrated in the appearance of the children. Only in the modern one do any children wear glasses which is one of the interesting comparisons you can make.

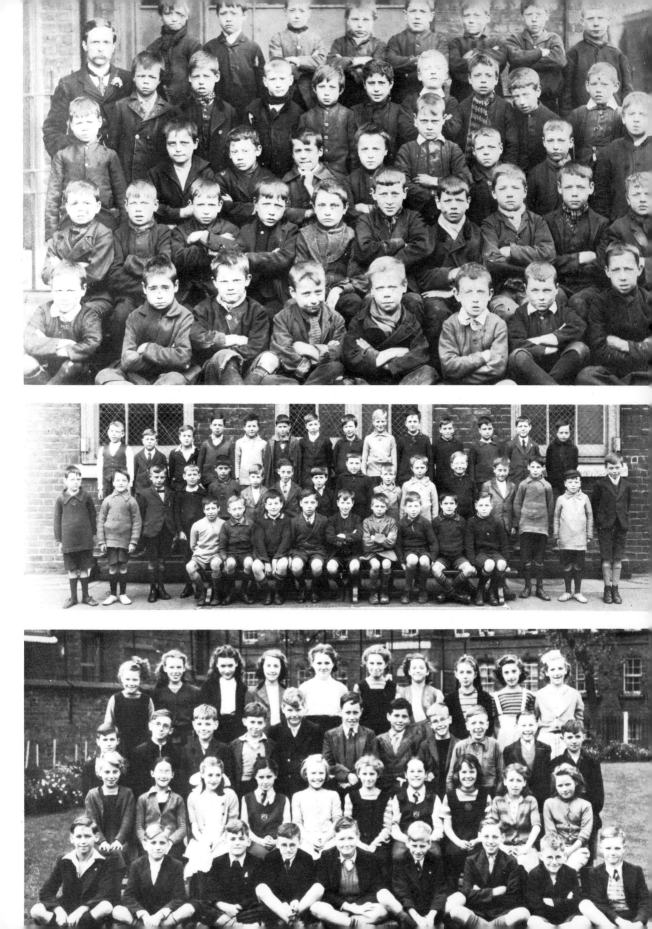

9 Holidays in 1923—a middle class privilege.

the national income. Their standard of living rises as they get their car, holiday, better furniture and so on. There is no evidence that the children of the working mother suffer in any way; on the contrary the evidence suggests that they may be healthier and enjoy better home facilities, so helping to make them better students.

The domesticated father
In the past the father was very much the head of the family. But as the number of domestic servants decreased so more fathers had to play a part in running the middle class homes. As the number of working mothers has increased so the part played by fathers in their families has changed. The father is now more conscious of being an equal partner with his wife—unlike his Victorian grandfather who knew that he was the head. This togetherness can only be for the good of the family.

EMPLOYMENT OF WOMEN
in Great Britain

10 A graph showing the increasing numbers of working women since 1950.

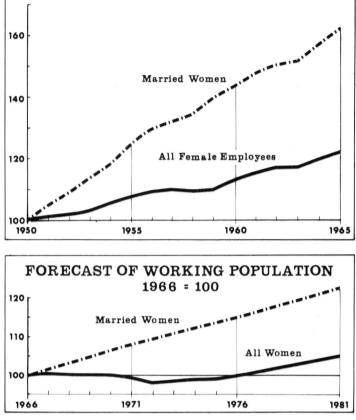

ESTIMATED NO. OF EMPLOYEES
1950 = 100

Married Women

All Female Employees

FORECAST OF WORKING POPULATION
1966 = 100

Married Women

All Women

Affluent families

Smaller families with larger incomes have become also much healthier families (Chapter 5, Picture 10). Women have been released from the burdens of home-making that faced their grandmothers and from the economic hardship that faced many of their mothers. These affluent women are able to enjoy a better life (Picture 5); their children too are able to enjoy a better life with their parents and in their schools. A comparison of children now and children in the same class in the past bears this out (Pictures 6–8).

Poor families

The country has become richer and more people are enjoying a higher standard of living reflected in their families' well-being. However, there are still millions of families whose joint income is still too low to allow them to share in this affluence: their housing is still very poor (Chapter 5, Picture 8); their clothing, food and furniture still far below that of the 'average' family (Chapter 7, Picture 10). The national income is still not being shared out sufficiently fairly to allow these people to enjoy the good life available to so many.

11 Evacuation 1939. Millions of children left their homes in towns and cities for safer war-time homes in the countryside and suburbs. Many people in the middle class suburbs met children from city centres and saw for themselves the results of poor housing, low wages, inadequate diet and other social evils. This was one of the driving forces behind the social revolution of the 1940s and 1950s; these middle class war-time foster parents wanted things to be changed for their visitors.

12 A woman operating a press for making concrete bricks in a South Wales brick works.

The Young Historian

1. Look again at Chapter 1, Picture 8; Chapter 2, Pictures 5, 7 and 8; Chapter 4, Picture 6; Chapter 5, Picture 6; Chapter 6, Picture 1. From these pictures make a list of jobs which are open to women.

2. Nearly half the married women in Britain go to work. How does this help to explain (i) falling mortality rates (Chapter 5, Picture 10) and (ii) an increase in the number of people owning their own cars (Chapter 4, Picture 3)?

3. In the 1930s many women voluntarily gave up working as domestic servants (Picture 2). Why? (See also Chapter 1, Picture 3 and Chapter 3, Picture 3). Many former domestic servants later went to work in factories, offices and shops. Why did they prefer that sort of job to being a servant?

4. Many homes have modern devices such as those in Picture 3. Why do such devices make it easier for a mother to run her home today? How does the existence of these devices prove that Britain is an affluent society?

5. What class of people went on outings in the 1920s (Picture 9)? Do you think that this is true today? Why?

6. Pictures 6–8 show children in the same class in the same school at different times in our history. Write a letter from the child in Picture 8 to a child in Picture 6 in which the modern child talks about (i) school (ii) going to work (iii) holidays.

7. In Picture 4 we can see that modern families are much smaller than nineteenth century families. How has this affected (i) the health of mothers (ii) their chances of going to work?

10 Education

By 1914 there were a number of independent boarding and preparatory schools for the children of the wealthier classes. Since 1914 there has been a steady increase in the number of such independent schools; in the inter-war period many people gained from the fall in the cost of living (Chapter 3, Picture 3 and Chapter 1, Picture 3) and some of them spent money on paying fees for their children. Since 1945, as the country has become richer, a large number of people have decided to spend part of their new wealth in this way.

By 1914 the local councils had begun to support some of the old grammar schools and had started to build some grammar schools of their own. These were fee-paying schools for day pupils, although any school which received grants from the government or the local education authority had to keep twenty-five per cent of its places open as 'free' places for the clever children from the elementary schools (Book 2, Chapter 10).

The elementary schools were either Church schools (Picture 1), or schools built and maintained by the local education authority. By 1914 every child had to attend school from the age of five until the age of twelve; most of the middle class children went to the fee-paying schools; the elementary schools were meant for the working classes. In 1918 the Education Act raised the school leaving age to fourteen so that the majority of working-class children went into a school at the age of five and remained there until they were fourteen while a handful of them left at the age of eleven to join the middle class children in the grammar schools, where they stayed on until they were sixteen or eighteen. As John Gunther, an American writer, noted: '. . . if a boy's father was a coal miner the chances were that the youngster would follow him; only exceptionally gifted, aggressive or lucky children emerged from their environment.'

1 An old elementary school to which children went at the age of five and from which only the few escaped at eleven to go to grammar (secondary) school.

2 Many new schools were built in the 1930s. This is a secondary school class in geography, in 1935.

The 1918 Education Act proposed the setting up of nursery schools for children aged three, and of county colleges, to which young workpeople could go for a day or so every week to continue their education after they had left school. However, with the coming of the depression in 1921 the government and the local education authorities and the employers were unwilling to let the young people have a day a week off, or to spend the money needed for the nursery schools or the county colleges.

In 1926 a Government Committee under the chairmanship of Sir William Hadow reported on the system of State education. It suggested that there was strong evidence that an examination when a child was eleven could pick out those children best suited to a grammar school education and that for the 'failures' there should be another sort of secondary education in a different school. Local education authorities were encouraged to build new secondary schools (Picture 2) to which the 'failures' would go after their eleven plus exam. By 1939 over two-thirds of the country's children were in such schools. As well as introducing a new type of school, the government and the universities encouraged teachers to start new subjects in the classroom; science (Picture 4), modern languages and music were developed during this period.

3 Old-fashioned drill (now P.E.) lessons in the school hall.

4 A science class at Tulse Hill School—an example of educational progress since the First World War. We no longer believe that education is concerned only with the three Rs of reading, writing, and 'rithmetic.

The evacuation of children from the cities and industrial towns, brought many middle class people into contact with working class children for the first time. They were shocked at the quality of these children's clothing, diet and health, and these middle class people were among the main supporters of Sir William Beveridge. In keeping with this spirit of reform, R. A. Butler brought in the 1944 Education Act which abolished fee-paying in grammar schools and said that every child would in future go to a primary school until the age of eleven, and then go on to a secondary school of one sort or another. The school leaving age was to be raised to fifteen as soon as possible (in 1947) and later to sixteen.

Mrs Chetwynd taught in a secondary school in the South London area in 1946. Parents told her:

'Living conditions are far better; no comparison with before the war. You can afford to care about schooling when there's enough food, clothes and the rent's been paid.'

'The war showed us the chances a good education gave. Not only commissions, but all the interesting jobs.'

'You worked alongside people you had hardly ever spoken to before, doctors, lawyers, civil servants. Sometimes there would be arguments about politics,

5 One of the many primary schools built in the 1950s.

6 Schoolchildren from a pre-war slum school in which too many of our children are still taught today. The teachers of these children had a much more difficult time than teachers in newer schools, and children were less attracted to school than are children in schools like the one in picture 5.

7 One of Britain's modern comprehensive schools in which some people hope to provide equal secondary education for all.

8 A more advanced society needs an ever increasing number of trained people. In the 1950s and 1960s a number of new Polytechnics and Universities were opened. This one at Bath was a College of Advanced Technology which has now become one of Britain's newest universities.

music and religion. You would realise how lucky people were if they had been educated, and make up your mind to see that your children had a decent education.'

'When this Education Act was passed, it sounded as though all the MPs agreed it hadn't been fair that everyone except the very clever had to have money to buy a good education. When fees were ended, we knew many of our children would be able to get into the grammar schools.'

'It just didn't work out. In a street there are a dozen children approaching eleven-plus who have been friends since they were five. Probably all the parents are hoping their child will get to grammar school. Primary school head teachers are asked to provide a great deal of English, arithmetic and even intelligence, for many people believe this can be taught. Parents compare marks, help with home-work, arrange extra coaching. Then, after the exam, three or four lucky boys and girls go to the school everyone wants, and the rest, who have failed, go to the other schools.'

Parents were very happy with the development of the new primary schools (Picture 5) in which their children enjoyed a great deal of freedom compared with life in the old elementary schools (Picture 1). But the parents were less happy with the secondary system. The selection of children at the age of eleven seemed to have too many faults in it. One child in three in Merionethshire 'passed' the exam. and went to the grammar school but only one child in eight 'passed' in Surrey; children from middle class homes with parents who had been to grammar schools did better in the eleven-plus than children from working class homes. A number of Reports showed that the selection system was not choosing the country's most able children—and when local education authorities allowed children in their secondary modern schools to take GCE they found that many of these 'failures' did better than the 'passes'—although according to the selection system theory all the GCE children had been picked out at the age of eleven.

Dissatisfaction with selection led many local authorities to build some sort of comprehensive school (Picture 7) for children at the age of eleven; all the children of an area go on together from their primary schools without any 'passing' or 'failing'. It is too soon, yet, to know how successful this system is but there is evidence that for many people it has been a success.

9 Imperial College, London, Britain's leading college for science and technology.

The head of a Maths Department in one school said:

'I have now found so many capable of enjoying maths that we've got about three times the national average in O-levels and should give five times the average in A-levels. Children who wouldn't have been given a chance in another school respond to the fact that the sky's the limit.'

Lynn Teasdale, who came from Hampshire, had failed the 11-plus and 12-plus and entered a low stream. Suddenly she discovered science.

'Straight away I just understood it. It seemed logical all the way through and that was it.' Next year she will go to university. 'At my old school I'd have left at 15. I wouldn't have taken O-level at all. And there were people at my old school better than me.

As industry became more automated so there was a need for more highly qualified people to build, design and maintain the new machinery. This has led to the creation of many new Universities as well as to the opening of a new form of higher education—the Colleges of Advanced Technology (Picture 8). Each year a higher proportion of pupils go on to some form of higher education, helped by government grants. A richer country can afford to build the new schools and Colleges and to pay the increasing numbers of teachers and lecturers as well as to give generous grants to students. A richer country has to be able to afford to do this because it needs an ever-increasing number of trained and qualified work-people of all descriptions.

However, there are still millions of children going to schools that were built in the nineteenth century. Some of these are schools in rural areas but many of them are schools in the older parts of the industrial cities and towns. All too often the children in these schools are the children who are also badly housed (Chapter 5, Picture 8), and whose parents are badly paid (Chapter 7, Picture 10). The quality of these children's lives is much lower than that of the children of the affluent majority.

The Young Historian

1. You may find that there is an old school near your home (Picture 1). Compare such a school with a new one with regard to (i) its outward appearance (ii) the playing space available for the children.
2. Many children still go to very old schools. Write a letter from a child in Picture 6 in such a school to a child in a new school (Picture 7) comparing their school life. Why will improvements in school buildings lead to an increase in taxation?

3. From Chapter 1, Picture 7 and Chapter 2, Pictures 2, 4 and 7, explain why the country has to have more technologists now than in 1945. Fine out the names of three Colleges of Advanced Technology (Picture 8).

4. In Picture 3 you can see children doing PE lessons. Write a paragraph by a child in the class, in which he or she says what the lesson was like and compare it with your PE lessons.

5. In the 1930s many new secondary schools were built (Picture 2). Why are there more comprehensive schools (Picture 7) being built in the 1960s?

6. More and more children are staying on at school after the age of sixteen. Why can their parents allow them to do so? Why did many children not get this chance in the 1920s and 1930s?

7. In Pictures 1 and 6 you can see an elementary school and elementary school-children. What was an elementary school? Why had some children left these schools at the age of eleven?

8. Music, science (Picture 5) and other new subjects were added to the school timetable in the 1920s and 1930s. Do you think that we'd be better off if we went back to teaching only reading, writing and arithmetic in highly disciplined schools?

11 Leisure

During the past sixty years Britain has become a richer country, her national income growing almost every year. This growing income has been shared out more fairly than was the case in the nineteenth century. There are many proofs both of the increased wealth and the fairer sharing out; more people are better housed now than in the past (compare the pictures in Chapter 5 of Books 1, 2 and 3). The majority of the people are better clothed (see pictures in each of the three books) and in the last twenty years an ever-increasing number of people have bought cars (Chapter 4, Picture 3) as well as household luxuries such as refrigerators, washing machines and so on.

One of the best ways in which we can study the growth of the nation's income and its distribution is to compare the ways in which people spend their leisure time at different periods. In Book 1, Chapter 11, we saw that the majority of the population spent their little free time and money on brutal forms of entertainment. Even at the end of the nineteenth century (Book 2, Chapter 11), there were

1   The interior of a television studio with its complicated and costly machinery.

2 Outside broadcasting brings sporting and other events into people's homes.

millions of people whose only form of entertainment was the street musician or band. One of the great changes that have taken place in the last sixty years is that more people have more leisure time than before and more of them have enough money to be able to enjoy this leisure time as they wish.

By 1914 the government had passed the Bank Holidays Act and many firms allowed their workpeople to finish work at 2.00 pm on Saturday. But the mass of the people had no holiday as we understand it; the middle classes might go to Scarborough (Book 2, Chapter 11, Picture 4), for a week or so; the upper classes

3 Caravans at Treco Bay, Porthcawl, South Wales, where thousands of people escape from their homes to enjoy the sea.

4 The decline of the habit of cinema going has been accompanied by the growth of the habit of playing Bingo—in the former cinema.

might go to Europe or Africa for a longer holiday; the working classes had no holidays apart from the Bank Holidays.

Within the last sixty years this has changed. An increasing number of middle class people became sufficiently well-off to copy the habits of the upper classes of the 1930s—helped by falling prices (Chapter 3, Picture 3). They, too, learned to go abroad, and shipping companies and tourist agencies expanded to cater for these people. Some of the lower middle classes and skilled working class could afford to tour the country (Picture 3) while many of them learned to imitate the middle classes and take a holiday by the seaside. By 1936 about one million trade unionists had won a week's holiday with pay from their employers and to cater for these Billy Butlin opened the first of his seaside holiday camps in 1937 (Picture 6). In 1938 the government passed the Holidays-with-Pay Act which did not force, but encouraged, employers to give their workpeople a week's paid holiday each year. Even in 1947 less than six million people had this privilege but by 1972 over half the working population has three weeks paid holiday; British industry can afford to allow people to take this time off because in the remaining working weeks, using more modern machinery, the workpeople produce more than their fathers did in a longer working year.

At first these new holiday makers stayed in Britain; they went to the seaside: Blackpool, Clacton and other towns developed new industries to cater for them. In the 1950s they learned to travel further afield—in Britain at first, so that Cornwall and Scotland became their holiday centres. In the 1960s the affluent workers had learned to imitate the upper classes and had begun to take overseas holidays. In all this they have been helped not only by their own increasing wealth (Chapter 7, Picture 7), but by the motor car (Chapter 4, Picture 3), the caravan (Picture 3) and by the many tourist agencies which have grown up to help people to spend their holidays abroad.

At home

The wealthier British people have also been helped by a series of technological developments which have altered their leisure habits. The development of a cheap newspaper by Lord Northcliffe meant that the lower middle classes were buying a daily paper in 1900; as his competitors imitated him and produced a larger number of cheap newspapers, and as the working population could afford to spend a penny a day on a paper, so in the 1930s an increasing number of people learned to read a daily paper—although it was not until 1947–8 that the sale of

5 Outdoor sport continues to be one of Britain's main leisure pursuits. Spectator sports are now less important than they were; more people are 'doing their own thing'; but football matches continue to attract huge crowds.

6 Billy Butlin opened his first holiday camp in 1937; as people became more affluent and able to afford holidays Butlin and others have opened more camps. This is the Butlin camp at Skegness.

daily papers reached the level of the sale of Sunday papers. Allen Lane founded the Penguin Press in 1935 and people learned to buy books for 6d; as his idea proved profitable so other firms were set up to produce 'Pan', 'Mayflower', 'Corgi' and other paperbacks on every subject from algebra to Zen Buddhism.

But the three greatest developments have been the invention of radio, television (Picture 1) and cheap, long-playing records. Now a vast audience can enjoy serious music or a commenatary on an event happening far away (Picture 2), as well as drama, comedy and so on.

Outside the home

During the 1920s the film industry developed and large audiences went to small halls to see silent films and learned to love Mary Pickford and Charlie Chaplin; when 'the talkies' were invented in 1928 the cinema began to replace the Music

7 In the 1930s the cinema was the means of escape from the harsh life of the depression. Cinema owners built 'Palaces' and 'Plazas', 'Majestics' and, as illustrated here, 'Granadas'. The very names were invitations to a dreamy world of wonderland.

8 Groups dominated the pop music scene in the 1960s and early 1970s. One of the most popular with young people were the Rolling Stones *(above)*. They were less popular with older people.

Hall (Book 2, Chapter 11, Picture 7) and the theatre as a source of entertainment. To cater for the large audiences many huge and luxurious cinemas were built in the 1930s (Picture 7), most of them having romantic-sounding names. Since 1950 many of these cinemas have had to close or to change over to being Bingo Halls (Picture 4), and people have learned to enjoy other forms of entertainment.

Male entertainment

As in the eighteenth and nineteenth centuries, the pub has remained a source of entertainment, although there have been a number of changes even here. There are fewer pubs now than in 1900 as more people spend more time in their pleasanter homes, watching television. Many of the pubs remaining have been redecorated to try and attract a younger clientele—male and female—while in the 1960s an increasing number of workingmen's clubs have expanded to provide music-hall kind of entertainment where singers, dancers and other artists appear.

In the 1930s and 1940s professional football attracted many millions (Picture 5): in the 1950s and 1960s the numbers of spectators has continued to drop as more men spend more time with their families, and families spend their weekends in the countryside (Picture 3). But the popularity of football took an upward turn in 1966 when England won the World Cup and the young football stars have replaced the film stars as young people's idols.

Do-it-Yourself

While the numbers of people watching films, soccer or cricket has continued to decline so the numbers of people playing individual games has grown; there are now millions of golfers, hundreds of thousands of people who own their own yachts and dinghies, thousands of members of clubs catering for enthusiastic rose growers or judo experts. It seems as if a more affluent people are also a more confident people, not only able to afford the price of participating but also willing to try to participate. It is a far cry from the street audiences of 1914 (Book 2, Chapter 11, Picture 8) to the working class people who try to copy world champion Tony Jacklin's swing, or Francis Chichester's expertise with a sailing boat.

9 An invitation to enjoy a variety of pursuits; golfing, sailing, foreign travel, skiing were once the privilege of the rich minority. Today the majority of the population enjoy one or other of these forms of entertainment.

The Young Historian

1 More people spend more time on entertainment than ever before. Give a list of the ways in which young people (up to 20 years of age) spend money on entertainment. What does this tell you about their families' incomes?

2. Butlin opened his first camp in 1937 (Picture 6). Why did the parents of small children welcome this development? Find out from an agency how much it costs today to go to Butlin's camps for a week's holiday.

3. You probably have a 1930s cinema (Picture 7) near your home. Find out the names of three such cinemas. Why were they so popular in the 1930s and why do fewer people go to the cinema today?

4. Many people go to watch outdoor sport such as cricket and football (Picture 5). What does this tell you about the country's system of transport and the people's wealth?

5. Look at Picture 1. What proof can you see that this country needs more and better qualified workpeople? Find out how much you have to pay for a television licence fee. Suggest five things that this fee has to be spent on.

6. Write a letter either to the BBC or ITV congratulating them on a recent programme which you enjoyed.

7. Picture 4 shows one caravan site in South Wales. Find out how much a new 4-berth caravan costs. There are thousands of caravan owners in Britain. What does this tell you about the standard of living ? Why do people pay so much for such caravans?

8. Draw or paint your own favourite holiday.

Neville Chamberlain,
1869–1940

Sir Winston Churchill,
1874–1965

Lord Atlee, 1883–1967

Sir Harold Macmillan

Lord Butler

Aneurin Bevan,
1897–1960

Sir Alexander Fleming,
1881–1955

Sir Geoffrey de Havilland

John Logie Baird,
1888–1946

Lord Northcliffe,
1865–1922

Sir Billy Butlin

Charlie Chaplin

Index

Numbers in **bold** type refer to pages on which illustrations appear.